DRAFTED

Cover photo courtesy of the author.

Bandido Charlie Command Track.
From left to right: Driver/author Ron "Bandido Mack"
Mackedanz, Gunner/ TC Al Kalchik, Company Commander
Captain Phillip J. Greenwell, II, Artillery FO Baby Fo,
and RTO Mike Renshaw.

DRAFTED

GREETINGS—YOU HAVE BEEN SELECTED BY YOUR FRIENDS AND NEIGHBORS

Ronald W. Mackedanz

P*

POLARIS PUBLICATIONS
An imprint of NORTH STAR PRESS OF ST. CLOUD, INC.
St. Cloud, MN

First Edition: November 1, 2012
Second Printing: March 2016

Printed in the United States of America

Published by:
Polaris Publications
an imprint of
North Star Press of St. Cloud, Inc.
P.O. Box 451
St. Cloud, Minnesota 56302

www.northstarpress.com

DEDICATION AND ACKNOWLEDGEMENTS

This book is dedicated to the memories of:
SFC Lyle Mackedanz (MIA/POW April 21, 1968)
SP4 Michael J. Tessaro (KIA January 8, 1969) and
The 58,000+ men and women who lost their lives in Vietnam.

I would like to thank all of my family and friends who encouraged me during the time that I have been working on this story.

Special Thanks to:
Woody Goldberg, for the foreword and his bridge story.
Chelsey Whitcomb, Ruth Knepper, and others for editing.
Lisa Wendt, for helping to make my dream become a reality.

Thank you,

Ronald W. "Mack" Mackedanz

TABLE OF CONTENTS

PART TWO: HOME AGAIN

FOREWORD

Many Americans, especially Veterans, have not yet achieved closure from the physical, emotional, social, and political ramifications of the Vietnam War. Countless veterans each in their own way continue to struggle with the meaning of the war and its after effects. Ronald W. (Mack) Mackedanz has effectively charted his own course to reconciliation as set forth in his auto-biography entitled *Drafted: Greetings—You Have Been Selected by Your Friends and Neighbors.* This book is highly recommended to those who served in Vietnam and those who seek to better understand the residue of war and the burdens that many continue to bear, including from other wars in which Americans have been called to serve and continue to serve.

As a fellow Vietnam veteran and "friend" of the author, I am honored to commend this book penned by an awardee of the Silver Star, the Combat Infantryman's Badge, two Purple Hearts for wounds incurred from hostile enemy action, and the Army Commendation medal among other awards. Mack and I proudly served in Vietnam with C Company, 1st Battalion, 16th Infantry (Mechanized), of the First Infantry Division, a company known in the United States Army as "Bandido Charlie," proudly named with the enduring camaraderie of those of its predecessor in Vietnam, C Company, 5th Battalion, 60th Infantry of the 9th Infantry Division.

Mack, with a keen sense of detail, shares with us the course of life that took him from Minnesota as a "reluctant warrior," a "draftee" to the battle field as a mechanized infantryman in "a war with little glory," and beyond. He is forthcoming in sharing the personal challenges he faced and how he met them. For those who know not the horrific nature of war and its potential after-effects, and for those who experienced firsthand that of which the author writes, the reader hopefully will find understanding in what war can do to one's psyche and the challenges of mastering one's own fate, after the guns have gone silent. Mack acknowledges he is "doing quite well today," as are others his charted course has touched and helped along the way to personal reconciliation, as in the ability to cope and put the war in some context. His outreach to fellow veterans, the families of "fallen warriors" who paid the ultimate sacrifice, is legendary. With the support of Janet, his beloved wife and life-long partner, family, and fellow Vietnam Veterans, Mack continues to make the lives of others have special meaning, because he shares his own challenges with them and us in his writings. He epitomizes "noble service," putting the greater good before self.

Ronald W. (Mack) Mackedanz epitomizes the motto of the First Infantry Division: "No Mission Too Difficult; No Sacrifice Too Great; Duty First!" He has lived this creed, bringing comfort to those who lost loved ones in the war, and special friendship and compassion to those with whom he served. His poetry is masterful for its contribution to understanding the affects of combat. He proudly reminds each of us that "Bandidos are Forever!" We "Bandidos" and others will salute him for sharing this must-read of a book by a true patriot who did it his way in search of reconciliation. Let it be said, when our nation called Mack and others to duty, each did their part—they served!

Sherwood (Woody) D. Goldberg, Esquire
Commanding Officer, C Company, 1/16 Infantry (Mechanized)
November 1968—March 1969

AUTHOR'S INTRODUCTION

THIS BOOK IS THE TRUE STORY of what is was like being a product of the Baby Boom, growing up in a fast-changing world, and being a small spoke in the big green wheel of a very unpopular war. It's also about surviving the war, only to return to a country full of anti-war sentiment and great disdain for its own young men that they had sent off to war.

These are the memoirs of a man who has answered his country's call, served as an infantryman for one full year in the jungles, rice paddies, and rubber plantations of South Vietnam. I have "seen the elephant," having faced death several times during my year with Bandido Charlie Company, 1st Battalion 16th Infantry (mechanized).

I walk you through my military career. From receiving my draft notice, through basic training, Advanced Infantry Training, shipping over to Vietnam, my first firefight, seeing buddies die, being wounded twice, surviving 363 days in 'Nam, coming home, playing war games in the snow, and finally, being discharged after two years of service.

I continue with the book, sharing with you what it was like coming back to civilian life, trying to find work, taking advantage of the GI bill, and always dealing with the stigma of Vietnam. Back in the '70s, '80s and early '90s, the VA was not very receptive to the Vietnam veterans. They had their hands full with the aging WWII and Korean War veterans. Then came the first decade of the twenty-first century when they finally figured out that PTSD was real, and many soldiers from all wars had been silently suffering with it for many years.

Through the years, most of our society, including a large number of WWII and Korean War veterans, turned a deaf ear to the Vietnam veterans. Many referred to us as "cry babies" due to the fact that we didn't just come home, roll over and play dead. Our government had promised us that they would take care of those of us who had faithfully served, and we were going to do everything we could to see to it that they lived up to their promise.

As time has shown, the determination of the Vietnam veterans has enhanced the medical care that is currently being received by all veterans, including the surviving WWII and Korean War veterans. Today, our servicemen and women returning from Iraq and Afghanistan no longer have to wait twenty or thirty years to receive treatment for PTSD or other illnesses or injuries sustained in a combat zone. While there are still instances where the VA has allowed some returning servicemen and women to fall through the cracks, they are getting better.

If you are looking for a fictional story about the Vietnam War, this book is not for you. If you want to retrace the footsteps of one who has been there, done that, continue. I hope that after reading this memoir of a Vietnam veteran, you might be able to appreciate the sacrifices made by family, friends, and loved ones who have served in the United States Military.

For those who served with Bandido Charlie Company during the year I was there, this story is as accurate as I can remember. In some cases, stories were relayed to me by others, and I have taken them at their word. If anyone feels that things may have happened differently, just remember that forty years have gone by. Some memories may have become shaded. Anyone still harboring a grudge about something that happened forty years ago needs to let it go. Come to one of the reunions and join in the camaraderie.

To all the Bandidos and others who have served in foreign lands, WELCOME HOME.

The Author,
Ronald W. "Mack" Mackedanz

BANDIDOS WHO GAVE THEIR ALL
VIETNAM, JANUARY 1, 1967—MARCH 31, 1970

24 Jan. '67	PFC Thomas E. Van Houten*	Nutley, NJ	US 14E 075
09 Mar. '67	Sgt. Ross J. Walker*	St. Louis, MO	RA 16E 050
26 May '67	SP4 Paul D. Skelton II	Waco, TX	US 20E 124
29 Jul. '67	PFC Martin M. Hunt	Menlo Park, CA	US 24E 028
29 Jul. '67	Sgt. Hugh Norwood	Orange, TX	US 24E 037
30 Jul. '67	1st Lt. Larry A. Garner	Mulkeytown, IL	RE 24E 051
03 Aug. '67	Sgt. Boris R. Bentley	San Francisco, CA	US 24E 070
23 Aug. '67	PFC Michael P. Mosbach	New York City, NY	US 25E 034
07 Sep. '67	SP4 Charles G. Hamilton	Slaterville, NY	US 26E 025
18 Nov. '67	Sgt. Willie Reed	Prichard, AL	RA 30E 018
18 Nov. '67	Cpl. Harmon S. Stone, Jr.	Oregon, IL	US 30E 020
19 Dec. '67	Cpl. Gary L. Norman	Erie, PA	US 32E 026
17 Jan. '68	SFC Herley Ayer, Jr.	Kahoka, MO	RA 34E 061
17 Jan. '68	PFC Kenneth R. Belsar	McClellandtown, PA	US 34E 065
17 Jan. '68	PFC Ronald L. Stroomer	Auburn, WA	US 34E 062
05 Feb. '68	Cpl. Wayne L. Golon	Bergenfield, NJ	US 37E 035
05 Feb. '68	Sgt. Robert Torres	Philadelphia, PA	RA 37E 046
14 Feb. '68	Cpl. Charles A. Stoval	Gadsen, AL	US 39E 040
25 Feb. '68	Cpl. Maxie E. Ackerman	Saginaw, MI	US 41E 015
25 Feb. '68	Cpl. George D. Whitelaw	East Detroit, MI	US 41E 032
25 Feb. '68	2nd Lt. Gordon K. Hughes	Upper Sandusky, OH	RE 41E 022
25 Feb. '68	PFC Gearwin P. Tousey	Green Bay, WI	US 41E 027
26 Feb. '68	Sgt. Robert L. Watts	Jacksonville, IL	RA 41E 046
01 Mar. '68	PFC Earl I. Althouse	Myerstown, PA	US 42E 012
01 Mar. '68	PFC Gary L. Oliver	Ashland City, TN	US 42E 022
01 Mar. '68	PFC Walter L. Thompson	Fresno, CA	US 42E 025
02 Mar. '68	Cpl. Neil S. Thompson	Warren, MI	US 42E 042
07 Mar. '68	1st Lt. Richard D. Bahr	Newport News, VA	RE 43E 041
07 Mar. '68	Sgt. Edward R. Cordeau	Winthrop, MA	US 43E 042
07 Mar. '68	SP4 Kraig S. Hogan	Sunnyvale, CA	RA 43E 044
07 Mar. '68	PFC Theodore T. Leo	New York City, NY	US 43E 046
07 Mar. '68	PFC Ben McCoullough, Jr.	Wartrace, TN	US 43E 047

07 Mar. '68	PFC Lewis B. Wilson	Manchester, TN	US 43E 050
27 Mar. '68	SP4 Joseph E. Sintoni	Sagamore, MA	US 46E 050
09 Apr. '68	SSG Emery N. Poitrow*	Ashland, ME	RA 49E 005
10 May '68	Cpl. Richard J. Flores	Hanford, CA	RA 58E 007
10 May '68	CPT Edmund B. Scarborough	Belle Haven, VA	RA 58E 015
10 May '68	PFC Randolph R. Wilkins	Camden, NJ	RA 58E 017
13 May '68	**Cpl. Armond J. Stein, Jr.**	Donaldsonville, LA	US 60E 003
24 Jun. '68	Sgt. Ernest W. Garrett	Hiawassee, GA	US 55W 027
24 Jun. '68	Sgt. John A. Lafferty	New York City, NY	US 55W 029
24 Jun. '68	Cpl. Charles C. Pedrick II	Alameda, CA	RA 55W 030
26 Jun. '68	PFC Lawrence Jackson	Houston, TX	RA 54W 003
28 Jul. '68	Sgt. Fredrick J. Krupinski	Jersey City, NJ	RA 50W 024
16 Aug. '68	PFC Clayton C. Brannon*	Freeport, FL	US 48W 023
20 Sep. '68	PFC William R. Morledge	Emmet, ID	US 43W 048
21 Sep. '68	SP4 Douglas K. Baron	Campbell, CA	US 43W 051
05 Oct. '68	PFC George Flohr, Jr.	Huntington Park, CA	US 41W 011
09 Nov. '68	**PFC Larry W. Bowen**	**Cupertino, CA**	**US W39 L39**
09 Jan. '69	SP4 Michael Tessaro	Edwardsville, IL	US 35W 061
24 Mar. '69	Sgt. Allen R. Miller	Edmeston, NY	US 28W 026
06 May '69	PFC Walter A. Elam	New York City, NY	US 25W 015
05 Sep. '69	SP4 Arthur E. Wojahn	La Crosse, WI	US 18W 045
06 Nov. '69	Sgt. Charles B. Roller, Jr.*	Houston, TX	US 16W 040
19 Dec. '69	Sgt. Clyde R. Carrico*	Orofino, ID	US 15W 071
16 Jan. '70	PFC Richard L. Blowers	Los Angeles, CA	US 14W 037
18 Jan. '70	SP4 Donald L. Martin	Jackson, LA	US 14W 043

With the rare exception of a couple of Bandidos who died from non-combat related deaths, most of these young men died fighting for their buddies on the battlefields of Vietnam

PART ONE:
DRAFTED

Bandido Charlie insignia.
(Photo courtesy of the author's collection.)

1

THE LETTER

D ECEMBER 23, 1967, THE FIRST of two dreaded letters came. Janet and I were living in Whittier, California. We were about to celebrate our first wedding anniversary. Good old Uncle Sam sure knew how to throw a damper on the holiday season.

Although we were living in California, I had stayed with the draft board in Glencoe, Minnesota. I guess that I was hoping that they might misplace my file, being that I was living out of state. No such luck. I wasn't trying to evade the draft; I just wasn't all that gung-ho about going.

I had several older cousins who had all gone into the service, and my dad and three of his brothers had all served during WWII. Two of my great-grandfathers had served in Kaiser Wilhelm's Army before they were allowed to immigrate to America in the 1880's. So, if I was called, I would go and do what I had to do.

The letter that I received on December 23, 1967, requested my presence in Minneapolis, Minnesota, for a pre-induction physical. This was, I believe, to determine if I was healthy enough to die for my country. So, around January 15, 1968, Janet and I flew home for a week so that I could report, as ordered. We stayed with my folks, near Olivia, Minnesota. On the required date, we went to Glencoe to take a bus down to Minneapolis. Somewhat to my amazement, there were a quite a few of my old high school classmates on the bus.

I don't recall the exact date, but they poked and jabbed us and asked us a bunch of questions. When they got done, they just said, "You'll be hearing from us." While I was home, I went up to Willmar, and talked to the local Air Force recruiter, Tech. Sgt. Larry Peart. He ran me through a battery of written tests, which I did pretty well on. Sergeant Peart told me that he could get me into the Air Force within four to six weeks. The problem was that I would have to stay in Minnesota, and we had all of our things out in California.

We decided that we had to go back out to California and get our affairs in order. Sergeant Peart, who has been a good friend of mine now for a quite a number of years, sent my test results along with me. He recommended that I take them in to the local Air Force recruiter in California. When we got back out there, I promptly went down to the recruiting office to see what my chances were. The recruiting officer down there said, and I quote, "All of you S.O.Bs wait until you are about to get drafted, then you come running to the Air Force." Well, yeah! Up until then, joining any branch of the military hadn't been all that appealing to me. He then told me that the soonest he could get me in would be in six months. Evidently a few other guys had the same thoughts that I did. I told him to forget it, because I would be in 'Nam by then. So I went home and waited for the inevitable. On April 18, 1968, the second dreaded letter came. It said, "Greetings, you have been selected by your friends and neighbors for induction into the United States Army." What an honor. Too late, I realized that it was time to relocate and make new friends. Obviously, these folks didn't think all that highly of me. Oh well! A man's got to do what a man's got to do.

Janet and I spent the next couple of weeks taking our furniture and other personal goods to flea markets in the area. Plans were to get enough money to fly back to Minnesota. I sold our 1959 Ford Fairlane 500 convertible for $150.00. AAAGGGHHH! We shipped a few boxes home, and caught a plane back to Minnesota.

About the same time that I received my draft notice, we received word that my cousin, Lyle Mackedanz, was reported missing in action in Vietnam. Lyle was a crewmember on a heli-

Lyle Mackedanz
POW/MIA April 21, 1968.
Never forgotten.
(Photo courtesy of
Natashia Johnson.)

copter up near the A Shau Valley. The chopper went down in bad weather while on a mission. Reports stated that they were hit by anti-aircraft guns. There were some sketchy reports that Lyle may have survived the crash, and may have been taken prisoner of war by the North Vietnamese or the Viet Cong. None of this has ever been substantiated. Lyle remains missing in action even now, forty-some years later. His name is on the Vietnam Memorial Wall. Let us all remember him.

My orders were to report for induction on May 16, 1968. After receiving the news about Lyle, I knew that I had to go and do my part, whatever that was to be. To do otherwise, I would never be able to face my family and relatives again, much less would I ever be able to face myself in the mirror again.

My folks were living on a farm place just east of Olivia at this time. I remember a few days before having to report, I was sitting in the kitchen of the old farmhouse. I had a chair leaned back against the window, straddling the chair with my arms resting on its back. I was just sitting there thinking, and looking out at the peaceful countryside, trying not to think of where I would be in a few short months. My Dad came over, pulled up a chair and asked, "What are you thinking about, son?" I told him that I

Author's cousin, Lyle Mackedanz, with his wife, Carol, and baby girl,
Cindy, just prior to leaving on his second tour in Vietnam.
(Photo courtesy of Cindy Johnson.)

really didn't want to go, but if I could somehow keep my four
younger brothers from having to go, then maybe it would all be
worth it. Sounds kind of corny today, but that was my thinking
at the time.

As it turned out, my brother Greg tried to enlist while I was
in 'Nam. Due to the injuries he received when he was hit by a car
when he was little, the Army wouldn't take him. He was quite disappointed, as he really wanted to join. Our next brother, Loren,
ended up enlisting about the time that I got back from 'Nam.

On May 16, 1968, Janet and my folks took me over to Glencoe to report. Goodbyes are an S.O.B. What did the future hold
for us? Would we have a future? Hugs, kisses, handshakes, tears
and forced smiles, trying to be strong. We boarded the bus, like
cattle heading off to slaughter. The goodbyes would not get easier
over the next two years.

A few high school classmates of mine, David Blake, Jim Christensen, and Gary Bell, were on the bus, along with many others. Some of the guys were acting all cocky and ready to fight. Most just looked apprehensive about what might lie ahead. When we got to Minneapolis, they ran us through our induction physicals. After that, about thirty of us were sworn in. They asked if any of us wanted to volunteer to be drafted into the Marine Corps. A couple of guys stepped forward. Then the Sergeant in charge said, "I need two more for the Marines." No one else stepped forward. He then took two blank sheets of paper and randomly slipped them into the stack of orders on the table. Then he said, "Whoever's names are under the blank sheets will go to the Marines Corps." As luck would have it, my name was right above the blank sheet. Whew! One bullet dodged.

I had three high school friends who enlisted in the Marine Corps while we were in our senior year. Larry Koepp, Gary Hanson, and Tom Healy went down to Minneapolis with the plan to enlist under the two-year, 120-day delayed enlistment program. Somewhere along the line, Larry decided that they should go for four years or nothing. When they got back to Hutchinson, Minnesota, they had enlisted for four years. They went in shortly after graduation in the summer of 1966. Larry had tried to talk me into going with them, but I was in love, and decided not to go. All three of them ended up in Vietnam. Tom Healy was killed in combat near Con Tien. Larry and Gary both saw a lot of heavy action, and were wounded in action.

Just prior to my being drafted, while Janet and I were living in Whittier, California, Larry and Gary came up from Camp Pendleton and had dinner with us. It was great to see them, even then as I was getting close to following in their footsteps. The thought of it terrified me, knowing the odds of making it back alive. Both Larry and Gary were concerned about having to go back to 'Nam for a second tour. Not something that they looked forward to. As things turned out, they both finished out their hitches, stateside.

2

FORT CAMPBELL, HERE WE COME

AFTER OUR INDUCTION PHYSICALS AND swearing in, they bussed us over to the airport and flew us down to Fort Campbell, Kentucky. We arrived late at night and were warmly greeted by a drill sergeant and several corporals. In his own charismatic way, he expressed how happy he was to see us. He also told us that with his guidance and nurturing, he would turn us into fine young men of whom our mothers could be proud.

As I recall, his words were something like, "all right, you bunch of lowlife maggots, get off of my bus and fall in." Most of us didn't even know that "fall in" actually meant to line up. Then he commenced to tell us that we should forget about our wives, girlfriends, mothers, fathers, and other family. "From now on," he said, "I will be your mother, your father, your sister, your brother, and anybody else that you think you need. Don't worry about your wife or girlfriend. She's already stepping out with Jody." They really tried to make us feel good about being there. They wanted to disassociate us from anyone that we cared about. Then they would work on building us up as a spoke in the big green wheel. Funny thing is that after telling us to forget about family back home, they wouldn't hesitate to get on our cases about not writing home to our folks.

When we got to Fort Campbell, my bag with my shaving kit, a change of shorts, and other necessary items didn't show up. I spent the next few days bumming things off of other guys just to get cleaned up. The first few days were filled with all sorts of really neat things like tests, shots, indoctrination, uniform and fatigues issue, more shots, calisthenics, and more. As a kid, I was deathly afraid of shots. I dreaded the thought of having to get all of those shots during basic.

When we went for shots, they would march us through a building, down a hallway, with our sleeves rolled up. When we got to a designated spot, a medic would appear on each side of the hallway, and they'd usually nail us with a shot from each side. The Army was using the new pneumatic guns for shots. They worked pretty well, unless you happened to flinch when they were giving you the shot. Then it could rip the arm and cause severe pain.

We took a bunch of tests to determine where we would fit in to the big green machine. My test results showed that I qualified for fixed wing aircraft and helicopter flight schools. I found out, much later, that I had also qualified for OCS (Officer Candidate School). As interesting as these options were, they all required signing up for a four-year enlistment. I respectfully declined their generous offers. My thoughts were that with a four-year hitch, if I survived my first tour of duty in Vietnam, I was probably going back for a second. That was a prospect that was not at all appealing to me at the time. I had decided early on that if I was going to Vietnam, then I wanted to be responsible for as few guys as possible. Rumors were running rampant about second lieutenants and others being killed by so-called friendly fire. I didn't want to be put in a position of risking other men's lives. As time would prove out, it was probably the right decision for me.

After four or five days of orientation, we were awakened by the warm, soothing, gentle voices of our drill sergeant and his band of corporals. I believe that his words were something to the effect of, "Get up and grab your gear, you bunch of maggots. Fall in, now move it, move it!" Once we were all in formation, with our duffle bags loaded with all of our worldly possessions, we moved out. They marched/ran us from the orientation center over to our basic training company area. They yelled, screamed, and cussed at us all the way. Using their swagger sticks, they hit the duffle bags being carried by those who lagged behind. You would have thought that they were going to kill us all.

We finally got to our barracks at about two in the morning. Our accommodations were sparse, to say the least. Two-tier bunks, spaced about five feet apart, and footlockers at both ends of the bunks. Any thought of privacy was a thing of the past. As it turned out, so was sleep. At four in the morning, our drill sergeant and his corporals came in screaming and shouting obscenities, questioning our pedigrees and telling us to get dressed and to fall out. We had five minutes to get dressed, make our bunks, and get outside in formation.

The Army was very nice to us. They gave us all brand new boots and clothes. They cut our hair and even took pictures of us with our new look to send back and impress the folks at home. They fed us three meals a day and saw to it that we got plenty of exercise and darn little sleep. They did their best to make us forget about home and concentrate on being a soldier.

They worked on building up us skinny guys and trimming down the fat guys. Several of the guys who couldn't handle the rigors of training washed out and were sent home. Some got section eights (psychological discharges), but most of us just toughed it out. This was definitely a no-frills situation. Temptations of going AWOL were always there, but for most of us, it was not even an option. Our young, macho, red-blooded American pride would not even allow us to think about it. Sneaking over to the PX to buy some candy, gum, beer, or cigarettes was strictly forbidden during basic training. There were vans that patrolled the streets around the basic training areas that sold fresh pastries, soda pop, candy, cigarettes, and more. Lord have mercy on the poor trainee who got caught buying anything from what we called the "Pogie bait trucks." If somebody got caught screwing up, usually his whole platoon got disciplined for his error in judgment. Punishment was generally handed out in the manner of more PT (physical training) and/or extra duty for the entire platoon. Needless to say, the culprit responsible for the punishment was severely dealt with back in the barracks. Middle of the night blanket parties were the usual manner in which the individual was repaid by his fellow recruits for the extra duty.

Army basic training may not have been Marine boot camp, but it sure was no walk in the park either. Basic training in Fort Campbell involved lots of running, calisthenics, weapons, and classroom studying and exercises. A big share of our training involved one-on-one close order combat and bayonet training, using our weapons and fixed bayonets to impale the dummies that were supposed to be enemy soldiers.

Drill Sergeants would holler out, "There are only two kinds of bayonet fighters: the quick and the dead. Which one are you?" to which we all hollered back, "The quick, Drill Sergeant."

We also had pugil stick training, where they gave us each a wooden pole with padding on each end. Then they would have us get up on a plank that was elevated off the ground about four feet. The idea was to go at each other and fight until one or the other was knocked off the plank. Weighing in at a whopping 125 pounds and standing five-foot-eleven, I was outweighed by most of the guys in my outfit. That didn't seem to make much difference when it came to pugil stick fighting. I usually got my licks in on three or four guys before somebody would take me off the plank.

On Sunday afternoons at a company area not too far from ours, they had a boxing ring set up. Anybody who fancied himself as a boxer could challenge up. It was fun to watch these matches as some of them got pretty ferocious, but I never had the desire to step into the ring. The days were long and hard. Every so often we were given time and instructions to write home. I tried to write to Janet every day when I could. It was difficult being apart, having been married for just over a year and now faced with all sorts of uncertainty. It was hell, not knowing when, or if, we would ever see each other again.

Two of our drill sergeants that I recall were Sergeant Miller and Sergeant Maris, (both pseudonyms). Sgt. Miller was a Staff Sergeant, who had done a tour in 'Nam. He had a brand new 1968 Dodge Charger. When he drove it around near the company area, most of us were pretty envious. Sgt. Miller was a man who was well respected and somewhat feared by his men. As it turned out, he was a darn good instructor. Sgt. Maris on the other hand was a cocky little banty rooster type. We first met him during our second week of training. He came hobbling into the company area on a pair of crutches with his leg in a cast. Turned out that a couple of guys from a previous training cycle had decided to

Bernie Bretch (Glencoe, MN) and Ron Mackedanz.
Basic training, Fort Campbell, Kentucky, July 1968.
(Photo from the author's collection.)

even the score on the little sergeant who had been making their lives hell. They caught up with him out back of the NCO (Non-Commissioned Officers) club, and broke his leg in the process. He didn't seem to have learned much from his little session. As far as I know, the culprits were never identified.

The end of June and the first part of July were hot as blazes in Kentucky. One of our basic training companies had a couple of guys who died of heat stroke. After that, the drill sergeants started cutting us a bit of slack. During the heat of the day we would get plenty of water, and classes were held in the shade of the barracks. We did a lot of bayonet training, pugil stick training, and rifle qualification with the M-14, followed by lots of marching and running as the day cooled down. We marched to the rifle range, we marched to chow, we marched or ran everywhere. The first six weeks, the training was relentless.

At some point, I believe after the sixth week, we were allowed a twenty-four hour off-base pass. A lot of the married guys had their wives come down. Janet flew down and we spent a day and a night just being together again. The past six weeks had been the first time that we had been apart since our wedding day, December 29, 1966. Of course, the hard part was having to say goodbye again. That never got any easier. Janet went back home to Minnesota and I went to finish my basic training.

Toward the end of basic, I came down with some sort of a flu bug and ended up in the hospital for a few days. I was discharged from the hospital just in time to graduate with my class. One more day in the there and I would have had to go back through basic all over again. In hindsight, that might not have been a bad thing.

Around the middle of July, we graduated from basic training, and quite a few of us were promptly sent off to Fort Lewis, Washington, for A.I.T. (Advanced Infantry Training). Did this tell me anything? They flew us out of Fort Campbell in the late afternoon on some old four-engine prop plane. As we were flying over Oklahoma, one of the engines on the right wing of the plane flamed out. The pilot had no sooner shut that engine down when one of the engines on the left wing flamed out. About this time, I didn't think that I would have to worry about getting killed in Vietnam. The way things were going, we probably would never make it to Fort Lewis.

By the grace of God, we were close to Fort Sill, Oklahoma. We landed there and were herded onto a waiting plane to continue our adventure. For some of the guys, this had been their very first plane ride. What an initiation flight! The rest of the trip was pretty much uneventful.

3

ADVANCED INFANTRY TRAINING

WHAT PART OF THIS CHAPTER title don't you understand? I guess we all knew, when we got our orders for A.I.T., where we were going to end up. As for me, it came as no big surprise. I had accepted the fact that I was going to end up in a combat unit in Vietnam, right from the start. I never had any grand illusions about getting assigned to some cushy job, out of harm's way. None of this was fact—just a gut feeling on my part. When that draft notice came, I just had that feeling that I would end up in the infantry. What the coming year had in store for me was not so easy to put a finger on. Like most of the guys, we all had an underlying fear that we would not make it home alive. Worse yet was the fear of not coming back to our wives as whole men. Land mines, booby traps, and other implements of destruction had a way of tearing a young man's body apart. To make it through a year in combat, without falling prey to one of the many heinous pit falls, seemed all but impossible to a new recruit.

We arrived at Fort Lewis, Washington, on July 18, 1968. One of the most noticeable things was the lack of the suffocating heat that we had left behind in Kentucky. We were to find that A.I.T. was much more intense than basic training. The emphasis was on training us to kill the enemy, and hopefully staying alive long enough to make it home 365 days after arriving in 'Nam. I was assigned to my training company, D-1-3, along with several guys whom I had gotten to know in basic training. Larry Groves and his friend, James Hodges, both went through the entire train-

ing cycle with me. Later, they both went to 'Nam and were assigned to units other than mine.

Many of the things that they had us doing were close-
order hand-to-hand combat techniques, including Judo and other
forms of martial arts, and weapons familiarization with M-16's,
forty-five-caliber automatic pistols, M-60 machine guns, M-79
grenade launchers, LAW's (light anti-tank weapons), claymore
mines, hand grenades, explosives, and every other kind of
weapon that we might have cause to use during our time in 'Nam.
The more proficient we became with these weapons, the more
likely our chance of survival might be. Needless to say, most of
us took this training pretty seriously.

Larry Groves and Ron Mackedanz, M-60 machine gun training,
Fort Lewis, Washington. August 1968.
(Photo from the author's collection.)

Along with all the weapons training, they also tried to
teach us something about Vietnamese culture. They never did
give us enough training on any one thing to allow us to become
very proficient at it. It seemed like their main goal was to get us
through training as fast as they could, and get us over there to
build up the troop strength and replace all the guys who were

getting wounded or killed on a daily basis. One of the things that the drill instructors at Fort Lewis seemed to enjoy yelling at us was "You'll all be dead by Christmas!" Boy! If that wasn't a morale booster.

For most draftees, we had a two-year hitch to serve. It always seemed stupid to me that they didn't spend more time training us in the areas of our assignments, and less time after returning from 'Nam, playing war games in the snow, and waiting to get out of the Army. But I guess that was part of LBJ's (President Lyndon B. Johnson) and McNamara's plans. It didn't pay to spend too much time and money training us, as "we'd all be dead by Christmas" anyway. The higher-ups had a plan, and we just jumped through their hoops like a bunch of trained puppy dogs. A few more months of training just may have helped to keep some of our guys alive. My thoughts on all this was that with the state of the economy, and the lack of jobs, the Vietnam War was just a retroactive abortion program for the middle class baby boomers. Hell, we ain't got jobs enough to go around, let's just get a good war going. That ought to take care of a bunch of those non-college guys that we don't have jobs for.

Be that as it may, we promptly followed our instructions like good little boys, and went off to answer our country's call, some of us scared shitless about what lay ahead, some of us cocky and ready to get over there and kill all those little commies, most of us proud that we were doing as our fathers had done before us: Answering our patriotic call and defending freedom, although not really knowing what fighting in a land 11,000 miles away had to do with our freedom. Only history and time would reveal that well-guarded secret.

The things that I most remember about A.I.T. are the nighttime navigation training, the live fire concentration course, and mostly, the opportunity to have my wife come out there for a month. The night navigation courses were set up so that we had to use a compass and any other means available to traverse about two miles of heavily wooded forest, with lots of undergrowth. It all sounded simple enough to a rural lad like me who had grown up fishing and hunting the vast wilderness of central and northern Minnesota. Little did we know that the forest contained squads of enemy soldiers, just waiting to take unsuspecting recruits off to a Viet Cong prison camp deep in the jungles, or the forest of Fort Lewis.

We were moving as quietly as possible through the woods, when one of the guys in our squad tripped over something. That something turned out to be an enemy soldier, lying in wait to spring an ambush on us (the enemy soldiers were guys from the previous cycle just ahead of us, who were being held over. Most of them were just waiting on orders). Before I could even react, two guys jumped me and threw me to the ground. Lying there with my face in the dirt and two guys on my back holding me down, I was at their mercy. They tied my hands behind my back, and then along with two other guys from my squad, we were blindfolded and marched to the prison camp.

Once they got us to the prison camp they took off our blindfolds, and for the first time in my life, I was looking at what a real life Viet Cong prison camp must have looked like. The officer in charge took our I.D. cards from us, and then they led us around the camp, showing us the snake pit, the hole, and various other places that we really didn't want to end up in. After about half an hour of showing us what would happen to us if we tried to escape, they untied our hands and put us in a wired off area to contemplate our fate. The guards kept making the rounds, checking on us every so often, making sure that we were not trying anything. Somebody should have told these goons that they were only playing the bad guys. Some of them really seemed to bask in the glory of trying to be the bad guys. They threw one guy, who was scared to death of snakes, into the snake pit. It really didn't matter to him that the snakes in there were non-poisonous. I thought the guy was going to either kill somebody, or have a heart attack. I never did let on that I was probably more scared of snakes than that other guy. It seemed that if the guards could pick out a weakness, they were on it like a pack of wild dogs. I just kept my mouth shut and my eyes open, looking for a way out. After a couple of hours, the guards seemed to not come around quite so often. I kept exploring the woven wire fence that surrounded us, hoping to find a hole that I could squeeze my skinny frame through. Finally, after working the wire for about an hour, I got an opening that I was sure that I could make it through. By now, the dark night had become even darker, as there was no moon on this cool late summer night.

Of the guys that were with me, there was a black guy named Dobson. I talked him into making the break with me. When the guards finished making their rounds and were on the other side of the compound, we squeezed through the wire and made a break for the woods. We weren't sure if there were other guards just outside the perimeter, or what might lie ahead of us. All we knew was that we were out of there, and didn't want to go back.

At one point, as we made our way quietly through the woods, I lost sight of Dobson. I whispered his name, and he whispered back, "Over here." I told him to smile so I could see his pearly white teeth. When he did, I could see that he was just a few feet away from me. After what seemed to be hours, we made it out to the road where buses were patrolling, picking up any stragglers. Boy! Were we glad to get out of there! The next morning, our drill sergeant asked how many of us had been captured. Not wanting to look bad, a few of us didn't raise our hand right away. He then told us that if we wanted our I.D. cards back we should probably come forward and get them. I guess they had us either way. It was a lesson that stuck with me my whole time in 'Nam. I just knew that I didn't want to end up in a real Viet Cong prison camp, deep in the jungles of Vietnam.

One of the really good things about A.I.T. was that if any of us married guys wanted to have our wives come out, they could stay if they could find housing off base. After talking with Larry Groves and James Hodges, we decided that maybe our wives could find a place and stay together. As it worked out, Janet came out, as did the other two wives. After about three days of looking for a place, the two southern girls were all ready to pack it in and hightail it back to momma. The third afternoon, Janet found a three-bedroom mobile home that they could get for the month.

Our platoon Drill Sergeant allowed us to go off post most any night that we didn't have some type of night training. We just had to make sure that we were back for reveille in the morning, or the privileges would be history. You can bet that we made it back on time each morning. Time has a way of erasing our memories, but I can only say that having Janet out there, and to be with her, was my whole world. We didn't know if I would get orders for 'Nam. Would I get a leave of absence before having to go? Would I ship out immediately after A.I.T? So many unanswered questions and time was running out.

Two weeks before I was finished with A.I.T. we were told that we should send our wives home, as the training was going to be very heavy from here on in. Living on a recruit's wages, money was really tight. I had to call my dad and ask him to send me money to buy bus fare for Janet to come home. A few days later, we were in Seattle preparing for her to board the bus for the journey home. This time, not unlike each of the last two times, the tears were hard to hold back. The chance of me going directly to 'Nam from Fort Lewis was a very distinct possibility. Again, thoughts raced through our minds. Would this be the last time that we would hold each other? The last kiss? Lord, please let it not be the case.

The last two weeks of training were very intense: a lot of night maneuvers, honing us to be trained killers, trying to prepare us for what we all knew in our hearts must lie ahead. The nighttime live fire concentration course was an experience most recruits will never forget. We were required to low-crawl under barbed wire and live machine gun fire, past exploding bunkers, and through dust and mud, bugs, and possibly snakes. If we jumped up, we would most likely be hit with machine gun fire. Just as I was finishing my turn through the course, one guy got up, just between the two machine guns (in a free area) and ran to the end of the course. One of the drill instructors saw him, and he made all of us go back through the course again. Had we caught that miserable low life, we would have definitely given him a darn good beating with a blanket party that night. Lucky for him, we never found out who it was.

The remark "You'll all be dead by Christmas" didn't seem quite so frequent now, as the possible reality of it was drawing near. Anxious to finish A.I.T. but not all that excited about what lay ahead, we all lined up to get our orders. Most of us got orders for 'Nam. A few of the lucky ones (probably enlistees) got orders for Germany, Korea, or stateside duty. My orders were bitter-sweet: Vietnam, but thirty days at home first. Thank you, Lord.

4

ORDERS IN HAND

O N SEPTEMBER 14, 1968, WITH my orders to report for deployment to Vietnam in my hand, I returned home to Minnesota to spend what would likely be my last visit there. Pessimism was something that was very difficult to put aside, especially in light of the current situation in 'Nam. President Johnson had increased the troop strength to over 500,000 Americans, and every day on the news there were reports of the many U.S. troops that were being wounded or killed in action. Also, in over five months, there had been no word on my cousin Lyle, missing in action since April 21, 1968.

My memory doesn't provide me with much of what we did during that month that I was home on leave. Funny how sometimes we don't remember the good things. It does seem to me that we had a bunch of the relatives over for a family reunion of sorts, although it seemed that it was more of a farewell to the doomed. All I really remember is that the month went by way too fast. My wife, Janet, and I spent just about every hour together, not knowing if we would ever be together again. Although I tried not to think about it, I wondered to myself, would she wait for me? I had to believe that she would, even though I knew that distance and time apart are very difficult on a marriage. I knew that I would do my best to be faithful to her, and I could only pray that she would do likewise. Only time would tell.

My orders were for me to report on October 12, 1968, to Travis Air Force Base, near San Francisco, for my flight to Vietnam. I had decided that I would stop by my sister's place in Alhambra, California, to say goodbye to her and her family. So I left home a day ahead of schedule so that I could do just that. My sister, Diane, and her husband had allowed Janet and I to stay with them when we were first married. Her two kids, Scott and Stacy, had become very special to my wife and I. As I recall, I only had time to spend the afternoon and early evening with them, prior to catching my flight up to Travis. I will always remember, as I was turning to walk out the door, my little four-year-old nephew, Scott, asking his mom, "Why does Uncle Ronnie have to go fight in the war, Mommy?" Out of the mouths of babes, they say. A question that none of us had a good answer for at the time.

I tried repeatedly to find the answer to that question many times over the next year. A war in a country that I knew very little about, for reasons that were very unclear to me. They kept telling us that we were fighting to stop Communist aggression, but what did we know about anything? We were just a bunch of naïve middle class American boys and men doing what we felt was expected of every red-blooded American who believed in freedom. Little did we know that most of us who made it back would be treated like the scum of the earth. Many guys would later be told upon arrival back in the states that it would be best not to wear their uniforms at the airport, due to the antiwar sentiment that was so prevalent on the West Coast.

When I arrived at Travis Air Force Base late on October 12, 1968, I was told to find a rack and to be at reveille at 0500 the next morning. Thinking that I would run into some of the guys that I went through Basic or A.I.T. with, I was quite disappointed when I didn't see any of them there. All morning long, we waited in large airplane hangars lined with benches as the staff there checked over our records. To my dismay, they called me and told me that I had not received some of the required shots that I needed. I guess that I had missed them when I went to the hospital during basic training. Lucky for me, they were all set up and prepared to rectify that oversight, and make sure that I would be inoculated against all the various medical situations that I might be exposed to. Most of the guys were getting two shots that day before deployment. Lucky me, I got five. My arms were so darn sore; I could barely scratch my backside. After getting my shot record all updated, I was sent back to the hangar to await the call for my impending flight to Vietnam.

There must have been about a hundred and fifty guys in that hangar, waiting to hear their names called and dreading the inevitable. I was seated toward the back of the room. When my name was called, I dutifully reported up front and received my flight number and seat assignment. As I was returning to my seat, a guy about two thirds of the way back, quietly said, "Hey Mackedanz, come over here for a minute." It turned out to be a guy from my hometown of Hutchinson, Minnesota.

LuWayne (Butch) Schuft was a brother to Chuck Schuft, whom I had graduated from high school with just two years prior. Butch was a year or two older than I, but our families had attended the same church for many years, so we kinda sorta knew each other from there. As it turned out, Butch and I, along with another friend of his, flew over to 'Nam together. As we filed on to the plane, each man was either alone with his thoughts, or trying to make light of a situation that we really didn't quite know how to handle.

The stewardesses, as they were referred to in those days, were very accommodating. Many of them had been working these flights to 'Nam for quite awhile. They knew that many of us were deep in thoughts of home and family that we might never see again. They also knew how to handle the rowdy guys, some trying to cop a feel or sneak a peek under their skirts as they were serving lunch and drinks to the guys. Those gals put up with a lot of stuff from some of the guys, but they were professionals at their jobs and knew how to deal with it all. Once we were off the ground and heading for our first stop in Honolulu, things seemed to quiet down for a while. Some of the guys played cards, while others read or just made small talk with the guys next to them. Still others tried to drink themselves into oblivion. Some even managed to catch a bit of sleep.

After about five or six hours of flying, we landed in Honolulu, Hawaii for refueling, and we got a chance to get out and stretch our legs. We were not allowed to leave the airport, but the three of us got some real food and sat around the beautiful tropical gardens. The sights, i.e. pretty girls, and the fragrant smell of the beautiful flowers, led one to almost think that he had died and gone to heaven. Compared to what awaited us, this was indeed a tropical paradise. We took a few pictures of us all in our khakies, and reboarded the plane for the next leg of our flight.

Ron Mackedanz and LuWayne (Butch) Schuft at Honolulu airport on the flight to Vietnam, October 1968.
(Photo from the author's collection.)

Having been on the plane, for over six hours already, this leg of the flight was somewhat quieter. More of the guys tried to sleep as others still worked on killing whatever brain cells they still had left that were functional. Having grown up around alcoholism, I had decided years before that I would do my best to try to stay clear of that. I always figured that life was enough of a challenge with a full set of brain cells; I sure wasn't going to handicap myself with booze and drugs. Some of the guys gave me some hassle about not having a drink or taking a hit of pot, but so what. They live their lives. I'll live mine.

On the flight over, Butch and his friend, Klawitter, and I got to know each other. We talked about the good times that we had growing up in small towns in rural Minnesota: playing sand lot baseball, swimming in the forbidden parts of the Crow River, in Hutchinson, delivering newspapers, and mowing lawns, along with the many, many other activities that used to occupy our young lives. We asked ourselves, how did we ever end up in this situation? Did we make somebody really mad? Or what did we do to deserve such a fate? No one seemed to have the answers, and realistically, I suppose that we never expected that anyone would have them. Most of us actually believed that our government would never lie to us. Looking back, were we a bunch of dreamers or what? A major reality check would soon be forthcoming.

Several hours later, we landed on Gooney Bird Island, also known as Guam. The island had to be one of the most desolate pieces of real estate that I had ever laid eyes on. It was nothing more than a long strip of endless sand, upon which the U.S. Air Force maintained a large landing strip. A few sparse buildings were all that broke up the monotonous landscape. This was the second and final refueling stop before heading for Vietnam. This time there was no place to get any real food or drink, so most of us just stayed in the area around the plane, stretching our legs from the cramped seats of the commercial airliner.

On the last leg of our flight, I could feel the apprehension building amongst the men. Not knowing what might lie ahead for each of us played heavily on us. The question kept playing over and over in our minds: Would we survive to ride the big silver freedom bird back to "the world"? Only the Lord knew the answer to that question, and he wasn't talking. At least, if he was, most of us were too preoccupied with our own thoughts to listen to Him. Little did we know that we were going to be put through a very tough test of our faith and our entire belief system that we grew up with. I guess that somebody should have told us in Basic or A.I.T. "There will be a test." Boy! That would have been an understatement!

All of a sudden, the Captain's voice came over the intercom. He told us that we were on our final approach to Saigon. I think that anybody could have bought the entire planeload of us for a nickel. None of us knew if we would get shot down on our approach, or if we would have to run for cover as soon as our feet hit the ground. The stewardesses did their best to be encouraging, wishing us all the best of luck, God's speed, and other nice things, all the while knowing that some of us would not be making the flight home. Who would they be? Did anyone really have any idea? What was to be our destiny?

5

TOUCH DOWN, VIETNAM

OCTOBER 15, 1968—REALITY SETS in. We are here, in Vietnam. The point of no return? A young soldier's mind runs wild. What fate is in store? Thoughts of the thousands who had been killed and seriously wounded in this Godforsaken piece of real estate. Thoughts of those captured by the enemy, including my cousin, Lyle Mackedanz, whose fate would, to this very day, remain unknown. Can I survive? How will I handle myself in the face of combat? Will my wife still be there when, and if, I make it home? Will I ever see my family again?

Stepping off of the commercial airliner at Tan Son Nhut airbase near Saigon, the first two things that hit me were the insufferable heat and the smell. Unlike anything that I had ever experienced, the stench of rotting, decaying human feces, along with the rest of the smells, were so nauseating that I almost felt like vomiting. Those first impressions of Vietnam would be locked away in my mind forever.

Not knowing what to expect, or when the shooting would start, the tension was strong as we boarded military transport buses. The windows were covered with wire mesh to deflect grenades or anything that might be thrown into the bus by passing "friendlies." The streets of Saigon were packed with locals. Some were on foot, some on bicycles or motorbikes, and even a few in cars, buses, and trucks. U.S. Military Police were on just about every city block. This entire scene reminded me of an anthill with ants going in every direction, with no obvious destination or purpose.

Vietnamese ox cart near Saigon, 1968
(Photo from the author's collection.)

Leaving Saigon, we bused over to Long Binh and Camp Alpha, the official welcoming headquarters for all incoming Army enlisted personnel coming to the country through Saigon. Camp Alpha would be our temporary home for a couple of days while we awaited our assignments to our units. The camp consisted of several one-story buildings, a mess hall, supply issue, an enlisted-men's club, and many barracks-type buildings to house the soldiers enroute to the real Vietnam. LuWayne Schuft and I somehow managed to stay together. Each day was filled with anticipation. Where would we end up? Would LuWayne and I be assigned to the same unit? What happened to all the other guys that I went through basic training and advanced infantry training with?

In an effort to keep us occupied, the sergeants at Camp Alpha had details for everyone. Things like kitchen patrol (KP), sorting gear at supply, cleaning up the camp area, and if we were real unlucky, we got the shit-burning detail. The U.S. Army, in an effort to not add to the ground and water pollution, decided that the new guys could pull the cut-down barrels of human waste out of the latrines, add diesel fuel and a match, and stir vigorously until the barrel was burned clean. If someone got caught screwing up in any way, they usually got that detail the following morning. Aw! That smell of burning feces permeating the entire camp area is something that I'll never forget.

LuWayne seemed to have a knack for dodging work details. One morning, he and I, along with about thirty other guys, were assigned to go to supply and sort through field gear. As we were being marched over to supply, there was a cart with a couple of acetylene cylinders sitting along the walkway. The sergeant in charge told LuWayne and I to move it out of the way. We didn't stop until we were about 200 yards away. By that time, the detail had entered the supply building and we headed for the club. Had we entered the supply building, our I.D. cards would have been held until after the detail.

That was the Army's way of catching us, if we happened to slip away before the detail was completed. Fortunately for LuWayne and I, they had not gotten our I.D. cards. We had the rest of the day to check out our new temporary surroundings.

Each morning, we were assembled and orders were given out to some for their unit assignment. On the third day, I received my orders. I was being assigned to the 1st Infantry Division, also known as "The Big Red One," headquartered just northeast of Saigon, at Di An (pronounced "Ze-on"). Little did I know that this was just a very temporary stop on my journey to my outfit, further north. As we sat on the tarmac runways waiting for our ride, dozens of choppers and troop carriers flew in and out. With the hustle and bustle of activity, it made me wonder where everything was going.

From Di An we went by plane, C-123s, to Lai Khe. There, I joined Charlie Company, 1st Battalion, 16th Infantry (Mechanized). Myself and about ten other new guys were put through some last minute jungle warfare training. Although we were relatively safe within the confines of Lai Khe, we thought that we might engage the enemy in a firefight at any given moment. At night, they would put us out on perimeter guard. There, we manned fortified bunkers with M-60 machine guns and our M-16s. We would sit there, watching and listening for any sign of enemy movement. We had several rows of concertina wire, claymore mines, trip flares, and other little deterrents to keep the bad guys out. It's amazing what tricks the mind can play in the middle of the night.

Mike Nelson, Caledonia, MN, at Headquarters for Bandido Charlie Company, 1st of the 16th, Lai Khe, Vietnam.
(Photo courtesy of Mike Nelson)

Most of the sights and sounds were nothing, but occasionally a trip flare would go off, and someone would fire a burst of machine gun rounds or trigger a claymore. That would immediately bring the whole perimeter to full alert.

Shortly after arriving in Lai Khe, our unit came in from the field for a couple of days of stand down. This was the first time that I had met real infantry soldiers. They all looked like they had been drug through hell, backwards. Many of these guys, in their late teens and early twenties, looked to be thirty years old or older. To say that they looked like death warmed over would be an understatement. A few days back at Lai Khe to resupply, have a few beers and some hot food, and we'd be mounting up for our next assignment.

Around October 25, 1968, with Captain Wendelin (Wendy) Winslow in command, we left Lai Khe with around twenty-five armed personnel carriers. Now loaded with fresh troops, along with the seasoned men, we headed north and then east to a place called Fire Base Jim.

Our mechanized company had just recently been reassigned to the 1st Infantry Division. In September, they had been brought up from the delta, south of Saigon. They had been part of the 9th Infantry Division. The unit had originally come over to 'Nam from Fort Riley, Kansas, as the 5th of the 60th Infantry. During 1967, Charlie Company, 5th of the 60th, under the command of Lt. Larry Garner, became known as "Bandido Charlie." The history of this company and the unit pride of having fought with Bandido Charlie is paralleled by very few.

In October 1968, a large number of the guys who had come up from the 9th Division were unhappy about the change. The 9th Division was a more loosely run outfit. The 1st Division had the idea of doing away with the Bandido Charlie name and calling the entire battalion "The Iron Rangers." Although this move was supposed to give the unit the pride of being associated with the 16th Infantry Rangers, it sort of backfired. The Bandidos felt that it was a slap in the face, and they were losing their unit identity that they had fought for. The Bandidos had just been through Tet Offensive of 1968 during the end of February and the first part of March. Then in May of '68, they once again played a major role in turning back what was to become known as mini-Tet.

Many combat engagements took place during that time, with the Bandidos losing twenty-seven of their men in combat, and many others wounded. Some went home, some came back out to the field, and some were reassigned to the rear or some other unit.

As I sat on the top of the 2-2 track (second squad—second platoon) waiting to leave Lai Khe, I had a lot to learn in a very short time. Most of the guys who had been in 'Nam for any amount of time had seen buddies killed or severely wounded. As a way of desensitizing themselves, they were not very interested in getting to know a bunch of new guys. The thought seemed to be, "Why should I? You'll probably just get killed. If I don't know you, it won't hurt me." and "Shit man, it don't mean nothin' anyway." The less we knew of someone, the less we could be hurt by their death. It was just a cold, hard way of insulating oneself from the inevitable. For the most part, the new guys kind of hung out together. We watched the old guys, and tried to learn what we could to keep us alive.

Second platoon Bandidos, preparing to move out.
Lai Khe, October 25, 1968.
(Photo from the author's collection.)

Bandido Charlie Company moving through the rubber plantation on
the way to FSB Jim, October 1968
(Photo from the author's collection.)

6

FIRE BASE JIM

A S WE HEADED OUT TOWARD Fire Base Jim, we had eight to ten guys
on each track. The driver and the fifty gunner always stayed
with the track. The rest of us were just grunts who rode rather
than walked. Not far out of Lai Khe, we came to the Suoi Ba Lang
River. An AVLB was brought up and laid a portable bridge across
the river. We proceeded to cross the bridge and headed east,
through the rubber plantation. Fire Base Jim was along Highway
1-A between the village of Phouc Vinh and Claymore Corner. The
terrain was predominately flat, with a mix of rubber tree plantations, rice paddies and jungle, along with some open areas of low
brush. Our job, as I understood it, was to work with the combat
engineers, doing mine sweeps of the dirt highway that went right
past our camp. Once the sweep was completed, we were to secure the road for the convoys transporting supplies further north
to other Army units in the northern part of III Corps.

On the mine sweeps, three or four combat engineers with
metal detectors would walk the road followed by some infantrymen on foot and then a couple of tracks. Five or six infantrymen
would fan out in an inverted V-formation, moving ahead of the
column. The idea was to look for wires leading to any command-
detonated mines, all the while keeping a sharp eye out for trip
wires for booby traps placed by the VC.

Fire Base Jim, as it turned out, was to be our base of operations for only about two weeks. During this time, I experienced
a lot of firsts as war raised its ugly head to meet me. The first week

33

there, a young soldier from California that I had become friends with tripped a VC booby trap. The word that I got was that he had been killed. However, in looking over the records of Charlie Company 1st of the 16th (mech), there are no reports of any of our guys being killed in action on or around that date. Misinformation seemed to be a constant companion. Through my entire time in 'Nam, people would come and go. Some of the wounded may have died days or weeks later. Some were sent home, back to the world. Some less severely wounded guys were reassigned to non-combat duty in rear areas. Friends today might be gone tomorrow with nary a clue as to what really happened to them.

Other firsts included seeing my first dead casualties of war, being in my first firefight (enemy contact), and going to check out suspected enemy base camps after the B-52 bombers and the F-4's had completely obliterated all signs of life from the area, pulling LP (listening post duty) out just beyond the concertina wire of our base camp on the darkest nights I had ever seen, and being on the receiving end of a VC mortar attack. We soon learned to isolate ourselves from certain things. If we didn't or couldn't, we'd never make it. The whole concept about respect for life seemed to change in a very short period of time. A lot of the South Vietnamese people seemed to give the impression that life was no big deal. You die, you die, so what?

As time went along and I saw guys in my platoon get killed or wounded, I tried to tell myself, "It don't mean nothing anyway." It seems that was just a way of trying to cope with things that most of us couldn't make any sense out of. I soon began to realize why the "old timers" behaved the way they did. By not letting anyone get too close, the loss would supposedly be eased. During those first weeks out in the boonies, we pulled convoy security along Highway 1-A. Trucks were loaded with ammo, fuel, food, water and every other sort of thing that needed to be transported to the outlying fire bases and villages.

We would position a track with part of a squad along each side of the road. On the west side, they would be about a quarter mile apart. On the east side, the spacing would be about the same, only they would be about halfway between the tracks on the west side, thus giving each track a good field of fire in the event that any VC would show up.

While sitting there waiting for the convoys to come through, the kids and the whores would come out from the village to beg or sell. Some of the guys, despite the repeated warnings, just couldn't leave the little brown girls alone. Most of these guys ended up going to see the medic and getting a shot or pills for the clap and other STDs.

With all the horror stories about the dreaded "black syphilis" and other incurable diseases, I wouldn't have messed with it, even if I had not been married. I soon learned that by showing the whores a baby picture of my wife that they would leave me alone. Thinking that the little girl in the picture was my daughter they would usually say something like, "Okay, you numba one *papa san*." They seemed to have some kind of respect for that, and they would be on their way.

One day in early November, as we were on convoy security, a couple of VC came sneaking through the undergrowth in the rubber plantation. Next thing I knew, all hell broke loose when the track just north of us opened up with their fifty-caliber machine gun and everything else they had. They killed one of the VC, but the other one, although wounded, managed to get away. Word had it that one of them was the boyfriend of one of the whores that had been out plying her trade. Supposedly, one of our guys had not paid her, so her boyfriend had come out to even the score. He didn't seem to understand that negotiating the price of female companionship was not going to be his area of expertise. His bloated body laid beside the road, like some road-killed animal, for over a week. The Vietnamese wouldn't claim him for fear of reprisal. The GIs wouldn't bury him because of the fear that the body might be booby-trapped. Every day that we passed by, his grotesque bloated corpse got bigger and bigger. One day, not being able to handle the stench any longer, some of our guys poured a can of diesel fuel on his remains, threw a match on it, and headed upwind. It seemed rather crude, but it was a way of dealing with a bad situation during bad times. Pictures of his decaying, bloated corpse and his charred bones, lying beside the road like some road-killed animal, still creep into my mind from time to time.

The apparent lack of respect for the dead, as well as the indifference toward life, were so foreign to most of us. I know that the Asian cultures have their own beliefs, but to a young red-blooded American boy, it was something that we never quite adjusted to. Many of the Vietnamese were Buddhist. Reincarnation was a part of their religious beliefs. If they died today, no sweat, they figured that they would be reincarnated and maybe come back to a better life. The other main religious group were the Catholics. Many of the South Vietnamese had been converted to Christianity by the French colonialists. Sometimes it was hard to figure, was this a religious war? A political war? A war against Communist aggression? I don't think that most of us knew who or what we were fighting for most of the time. The South Vietnamese didn't seem to care one way or the other.

After the convoys had gone through, we usually went out checking suspected VC or NVA base camps, tunnel complexes, or looking for supply caches. One morning we were told to get ready to roll out. Just after convoy patrol we would be heading over to the east. The B-52 bombers had hit a suspected NVA base camp about ten klicks to the east. We were going over to make a sweep of the area. As our column of APCs rumbled through the rubber plantation and jungle, I didn't know what to expect. About a mile or so from our objective we came to the Suoi Gpuc River. With no way of getting the tracks across, we dismounted and proceeded on foot. River crossings were always dangerous. Not only were we vulnerable to enemy attack, but the deep swift currents could easily pull us under. Our strongest swimmer was sent across with a rope while we covered him from the other side. Once he made it across and tied the rope off, the rest of us followed. Somewhat apprehensive, we each took our turn. Grabbing ahold of the rope, loaded down with full combat gear, we dropped right off the bank into the dark, deep murky water. Struggling to keep our heads and rifles above the water, we half swam, half pulled ourselves across to the other side. It's hard to do, loaded down with all the extra weight.

Once on the other side, we regrouped and proceeded cautiously to our objective. With each platoon in position, we started a sweep of the area. It looked like a picture straight out of hell. All the trees and other vegetation were completely gone, burned off by the napalm. Bomb craters twenty feet wide and eight to ten feet deep covered the entire area. The smell of napalm hung like burnt death in the air as we slowly, methodically made our way, looking for any sign of NVA activity. The bombs had done their job. There was no sign of anything even remotely human. As we moved though the area, the total devastation was almost unbelievable. The GIs looked like ghost soldiers, drifting through hell, as if looking for signs of lost souls. Was this to be a sneak preview of hell?

After sweeping the devastated target area and finding little to no sign of the NVA, we made our way back to the tracks. For most of us new guys this was our first real dismounted operation. Tension ran high as we returned to the waiting APCs, knowing that we were going to have to cross the river again, expecting all hell to break loose at any given moment. Once back to the tracks, we loaded up and headed back through the rubber plantation and FSB Jim.

About halfway back in the column, shots rang out. Scared half to death, I bailed off the track and took cover behind a rubber tree. Not being able to see anything, I held my fire. As I lay there between our track and that rubber tree, I realized that all my extra clips of ammo were still up on top of the track. The M-60 machine gunner threw the bandoleer of ammo down to me. This so-called firefight didn't last long. In the end, it was discovered that one of our guys back in the column had gotten a bit trigger happy and shot some poor little Vietnamese deer. Strange things happen when everybody is on edge. For some of us, this was our first exposure to what a firefight might be like. For a brief time, we thought that we were in it, big time. Real or imagined, the threat of death always hung in the air and rode with us wherever we went.

Fire Support Base Jim was located east of Lai Khe on the road to Phouc Vinh. Surrounded by nippa palm trees to the north, east and south, and open to the main road on the west, it was regularly hit by VC mortars every few days—usually in the evenings, just as we were preparing to send out our ambush patrols for the night. Those not going out on an ambush would find themselves on a listening post, just outside the wire, or on perimeter guard every few hours throughout the night.

Sleep was something that was somewhat elusive. We just learned to sleep when we could, often when taking turns on security as we waited for the convoys.

One day, during the first part of November, we got word to saddle up and roll out. The 2nd of the 28th (Black Lions) were in heavy contact with the NVA over in the Iron Triangle. The Bandidos were on the way.

Welcome to the Iron Triangle, November 1968. This sign was at the
river bridge crossing into the Iron Triangle, an area north and west of
Saigon where the VC and NVA staged prior to Tet of 1968. Large areas
of tunnel complexes were found in this area.
(Photo from the author's collection.)

7

THE IRON TRIANGLE

LED BY CAPTAIN WENDELIN (WENDY) Winslow, the Bandidos rolled down the road through Ben Cat to the Thi Tinh River, crossing the bridge into the Iron Triangle. Within a few kilometers west, we started to find dead North Vietnamese soldiers, with Black Lions patches placed randomly on their bodies. Huge caches of rice and munitions were found in the area and the Black Lions were in hot pursuit of the fleeing North Vietnamese soldiers.

That night, November 7, 1968, the Bandidos set up a night defensive perimeter. After sending out a few ambush patrols, those of us left with the tracks set about our guard duty with at least one of us awake and on guard on each track throughout the night. Shortly after dark, we took a few mortar rounds from the NVA who had eluded the Black Lions. One of our guys from the second platoon, Johnny Farley, got wounded with shrapnel from one of the mortar rounds. He was medevaced out, but returned to the field just a few days later. No ticket home for this one.

The next day, we broke camp and headed south through the jungle until we came to a rubber plantation. Right in the middle of the rubber plantation was a large clearing. This would be the Bandidos new home for a couple of months. We set about digging bunkers, filling sand bags, cutting trees for the bunker roofs, and stretching concertina wire to form a perimeter around our new Fire Support Base. Artillery was brought in by helicopter and extended the range of big guns deeper into the enemy stronghold.

Ron Mackedanz at FSB Huertgen, reading a letter from home.
November 1968.
(Photo from author's collection.)

Many nights we were sent out on three-man LPs just be-yond the wire. If enemy movement was heard, we would call it in, and then hope that we could make it back in through the wire without getting shot by our own guys, especially the 105s with their beehive rounds.

Frequently, we would leave the base camp, which was later named Fire Support Base Huertgen, in the early evening with a few armed personnel carriers. After traveling a few klicks, three of us would drop off, on the run, not wanting to give away our intended position for our nighttime LPs. The APCs would keep on going for a ways further before turning back for FSB Huertgen. Meanwhile, the three of us would make our way to a predetermined location where we would set up for the night. Once we got set up, we would call for the artillery to fire a mark-ing round within just a couple of hundred yards of our position. Lord help the LP that was not in the right spot. Once the marking rounds (known as dep cons) had been fired, we at least knew that we could call in artillery on the enemy if we got hit during the night. It might mean calling the rounds in on our own position if things got really bad.

The idea of these LPs was to monitor suspected NVA and VC trails, and to disrupt their activity with artillery. The U.S. military also had sensors that they had dropped along suspected trails that the VC and NVA would use. If these were triggered at night, artillery was given a fire mission to soften up the area of suspected activity. One night while trying to maintain absolute silence, one of our guys got a beetle in his ear. The darn thing tried gnawing its way deeper and deeper. All the while, the poor guy was just about going nuts. I thought that we were going to have to give him a horizontal butt stroke and knock him out, just to keep him quiet and not give away our position. The next morning our medic was able to extract the beetle from his ear. As far as I know, he had no long-term effects from his confrontation with the nasty little critter.

On another LP, we had a guy who was really bad at snoring. We had to keep waking him up every few minutes or he would have given our position away. Most of the time, the night passed without any sign of the bad guys. One of the biggest concerns while out on LP was that the guys assigned to stay awake for two hours might fall asleep and the VC would slip in and slit our throats. Shortly after daybreak we would gather up our things and move out to a predetermined location where we would meet up with our guys on the APCs. If we were lucky, we got a quick breakfast of C-rations while heading out on our next assignment.

During the last week of November and the first couple weeks in December, 1968, a lot of our time when not out on patrols, ambushes, or search and destroy missions was spent improving our positions at FSB Huertgen. One day while I was taking some equipment off the top of one of the APCs, a couple of F-4 Phantoms came over so low that they looked like I could see the rivets in the plane. Our Company Commander knew one of the pilots, who had just completed a bomb run, and he asked him to drop in and give us a fly over. They darn near blew me right off the top of the track.

The night of December 2, 1968, a couple of platoons of Charlie Company headed out on foot through the rubber trees east of FSB Huertgen for the village of AnDien. The plan was to do a cordon and search of the village at first light and rout out any suspected VC that might have made their way into the village during the night. Quietly, we surrounded the village with troops on all sides. At first light, a couple of squads went in and did a *hooch*-to-*hooch* search. A couple of VC tried to escape across the rice paddies on the north side of the village. When they ran into a couple of our guys hunkering down by a rice paddy dike, their luck ran out. Refusing to throw down their weapons, they were both shot and killed.

After the cordon and search were over, a General came flying in on a chopper and made a big deal out of it. He congratulated the guy who had shot the VC, gave him one of the SKS rifles to keep, and took the other one with him. Body count was an everyday thing with the higher ups. It was their way of keeping score.

Right about the time of the cordon and search of AnDien, we started doing rice denial patrols. The Vietnamese farmers were working to bring in the rice harvest, and the VC and the NVA were taking advantage of the abundant crop. Without the protection of the U.S. Army, the VC and NVA would just take what they needed from the South Vietnamese farmers. About the same time, one of the platoons from Bandido Charlie was assigned the task of protecting the village of AnDien. For some reason, they were replaced with the second platoon after a week or so.

We would go down by the rice paddies and set up with our tracks spaced a good distance apart. Most of the time we only had two or three of us on each track. This was pretty easy duty; usually one of us would keep watch while the other guys would

Rice harvest near AnDien, November 1968.
(Photos from the author's collection.)

kick back, read a book, take a much needed nap, or write letters home. Our presence kept the local VC from taking the rice away from the farmers. This was beneficial in two ways: one, it gave the farmers some crop to sell, and two, it deprived the VC and NVA of the much needed food supply.

Frequently, the kids from the village would come out and just hang around. One day, I had some Jiffy Pop popcorn that my wife had sent me. I broke off a piece of C4, lit it and commenced to heat up a batch of popcorn. There was a Vietnamese boy about eight or ten years old sitting there in the common squat position used by the peasant population. When the aluminum foil on the corn started to rise, he took off out of there like a streak of lightning. I think that he figured that it was going to blow up or something. He came back when he saw me eating the popcorn, and I gave him a handful or two.

The second platoon was the platoon that I was assigned to as a rifleman/RTO (radio/telephone operator). During a good share of December, my duties included serving as the RTO for our platoon leader, 1st Lieutenant John McCarthy. He was a big strapping guy, about 180 pounds, lean and fit. Most days, he would be carrying his forty-five-caliber pistol and little else. I, on the other hand, weighed in at about 130 pounds soaking wet. Carrying the PRC 25 radio, commonly known as "the Prick-25" and my full field gear, I had a hell of a time keeping up with Lt. McCarthy. I was glad when another new guy was finally assigned the task of being the RTO.

During this time, we were involved in a number of activities: winning the hearts and minds of the South Vietnamese population near AnDien, building our new platoon-sized fire base on the southwest side of AnDien, providing medical assistance, building playground equipment, digging wells, pulling security down at the village chief's *hooch*, and setting up ambushes in the rice paddies around the village at night. Some of these were with members of the local Ruff Puffs (local popular forces). Most often, on these ambush patrols, three or four GIs and eight to ten Ruff Puffs would set up an ambush.

If we got into any action, the Ruff Puffs would *di di* (run) back to the village, leaving us out there to handle the situation. Most of the time we weren't sure just which side the Ruff Puffs were on. We didn't have a lot of faith in their allegiance to the

South Vietnamese cause. Many nights, we laid in the rice paddies, behind dikes where it was mostly dry. We would set out our claymores facing the anticipated direction that the VC would come from. Frequently after dark, they would infiltrate the village. Some of them had family living there; others were coming in to take whatever they could to help sustain them out in the bush. Our mission was to intercept them and kill or capture them if possible. On occasion when we would spring an ambush, the following day we'd have some Vietnamese local show up at our Med-Caps with a gunshot wound. Wonder where the heck that came from?

One night, I and two other guys went down to provide security for the village chief and his family. His wife, an old *Mama San*, was holding her granddaughter and trying to rock her to sleep in a rocking chair on the dirt floor in front of their hooch. The little girl, about a year old, was fussing and crying. No way was she going to sleep. I went over to the old woman and asked

Ron Mackedanz, holding the village chief's granddaughter.
(Photo from the author's collection.)

her to give me the baby. She was very reluctant to do so. Finally I handed my rifle off to one of my buddies, and again asked her for the baby. This time she handed the little girl over to me. I sat down in the rocking chair and started humming the tune "Rock A Bye Baby." In a matter of minutes, the baby was sound asleep in my arms. The old *Mama San* couldn't believe it. I handed the little girl back to her and she took her inside and put her to bed. Every time after that when I was down in the village, the old *Mama San* would come up to me, pat me on the arm and say to me, "You, numba one *Papa San*, numba one." I always had a weak spot for the little kids even though they were on occasion used by the VC to kill and injure GIs who had come to trust these kids.

One night down in AnDien, we were providing security for the Psyops team out of Lai Khe. They were showing some movies, cartoons, and propaganda films on the side of a building when all of a sudden, there was an explosion as a hand grenade was dropped inside one of the Psyop's trucks. No one was ever apprehended, but several people saw a young boy running away just before the explosion. Fortunately, no one was injured or killed.

Christmas was coming and most of us were concerned about the Vietnamese New Year coming up around the end of January. On Christmas Eve, as the whole world was led to believe that we were enjoying a Christmas truce, a squad of us left the base camp at AnDien and headed down toward one of our APCs that had hit a mine while on rice denial patrol the previous day.

We were under strict orders to not initiate any contact with the enemy, but to return fire if fired upon. As it was getting dark, we quietly made our way down through the sparse vegetation, toward the destroyed track. About two hundred yards from our destination, we spotted a couple of VC with a block of crystallized TNT. It appeared that they were preparing to set it close to the destroyed track with hopes of possibly getting another track with their mine.

I don't recall if they fired first or not. It really didn't seem to matter much at that point. I was carrying the radio and my

M-16, along with my other gear. One of our guys with a thump gun (M-79 grenade launcher) fired a couple of rounds at the VC and all hell broke loose. I jumped into a small depression with our M-60 gunner, calling for support. I remember a rocket-propelled grenade landed just short of our position. Then one hit right behind us, narrowly missing us as it went just over our heads. All of a sudden, from behind us came two tracks with their fifty-caliber machine guns blasting away. Believe me, at that point in time, it was the best Christmas present that I could have asked for. "Silent Night" could not have sounded sweeter. We had a couple of our guys wounded, and we never did find any sign of dead or injured VC. Having compromised our position for the night, and hopefully having run the VC off, our ambush was scrapped.

The next couple of weeks were fairly quiet, as we continued reinforcing our platoon-sized base camp. A mortar squad was brought in and we were building a command bunker in the center of the area. Three or four guys from our platoon were sent down to Division HQ at Di An to bring back a couple of new APCs to replace a couple that were combat losses. Mike Nelson told me later that when they got down to Di An, the Bob Hope Show was on base. Mike and the other guys were in the EM club when a sergeant came in and told them to come with him. They were about the only guys in the club with dirty fatigues from being out in the bush. The Bob Hope Show was beginning and I guess that they thought it would look good to have a few guys in the audience who actually looked like they were in a war. The guys were ushered right up front, and Mike said that when Ann Margaret came out in her little yellow hot pants, they all got their eyes full. I never forgave him for his good fortune.

In my entire year in Vietnam, all I ever got to see were a couple of Vietnamese bands at the enlistedmens clubs in Lai Khe, Di An, and Da Nang the few times that I ever got back in the rear area. To this day, Mike and I still joke about that little episode whenever we get together.

Little did we know that before long, our peaceful little piece of the Vietnamese countryside would take a real turn for the worse. January 8, 1969, started out like most every other day. We pulled guard around our base camp, filled sand bags to finish off the command bunker that we were building, went down to the village, and worked on winning the hearts and minds of the local South Vietnamese. Later that evening, Mike Nelson and his squad went out on ambush patrol in the rice paddies about a mile from our base camp. A few others went down to the village to pull security. Shortly after dark, a heavy fog rolled in. Nels and his guys couldn't see more than just a few feet. As they lay there silently, straining their eyes for movement, a column of VC came walking on the very same paddy dike that they were laying by. They had their claymores set by the next dike over, so they were of no use. Not knowing how many VC there were, and not being able to see through the fog, they refrained from blowing their ambush. Hoping and praying that none of the VC would trip over their claymore wires, they waited as about thirty-five VC marched out of sight through the fog.

After a few minutes, assuming that all the VC were past, they radioed up to our base camp to let us know that the VC were heading our way. We got everyone in position: on the fifties, the M-60 machine guns, claymores, mortars, and everything we had. I was on a bunker that faced west toward a small wooded draw. We expected that this was the cover that the VC were using to close in on us. When the first shots came in, we were all set for them. We cut loose with everything we had. I was firing my M-16 at any muzzle flashes that I could see. All of a sudden, my left pant leg was wet. I thought that I had wet my pants. Later I found out that a piece of shrapnel had hit me in the back of my leg, and it was bleeding pretty good.

Shortly after discovering that I was hit, I headed over to the command bunker that was still under construction in the middle of the base camp. With the exception of some artillery illumination rounds, it was very dark. As I made my way down into the command bunker, I found Michael Tessaro laying there. He had been severely wounded when a rocket-propelled grenade hit the command bunker. I don't recall whether or not there were any other guys right there at the time or not. All I remember is that Michael was hurt really bad. I hollered for a medic, who got over to us and went to work on Michael. Things get a little gray from that point on.

The next thing that I remember is a dust-off chopper coming in to take out the wounded. There were about ten of us, as I recall. As they loaded us on the chopper, I was sitting by the door on the right hand side. They had Michael on a stretcher and loaded him in on the floor of the chopper. His head laid by my feet. As we rode into Lai Khe to the field hospital, I sat there looking at Michael, not knowing if he was alive or dead, and not

Michael Tessaro and Mesker Massey at FSB Huertgen
in the Iron Triangle. December 1968.
(Photo courtesy of Michael's family.)

knowing what to do for him if he was still alive. The shrapnel from the RPG had torn into his face and chest. I believe that he died on the flight in to Lai Khe. The next day I heard that he had died. The entire second platoon took his death pretty hard. Michael was one of those guys that everybody liked.

I don't know what went on after we were dusted off, but from what I was told, the enemy broke contact rather quickly after we answered their first volley with the full force of every weapon we had. I'm sure that they expected to find a camp that was being guarded by just a few sleepy guards. But when their first rounds came in, we cut loose with everything we had. The next day, while making a sweep of the draw west of camp, they found a wounded VC. He had a big chunk of his stomach missing, but he was sitting there, smoking a joint. I guess that the joint helped to ease the pain. I never heard what ever became of him; I just assumed that he died.

I was treated for my leg wound, given a shot, some iodine, and a bandage. The doctor told me that if they were to try to take the shrapnel out that they would have to cut my leg muscles to the point where I'd be out of action for quite awhile. Considering that we had lost a large number of guys recently through combat and rotations, they wanted to get me back out in the field as soon as possible.

So they left a chunk of metal in my leg about the size of a nine millimeter bullet. I still carry that little piece of shrapnel around in my left thigh. Along with that little souvenir, the Army presented me with my first Purple Heart. When I got back out in the field, a few of the guys started giving me crap about having been dusted-off without being hit all that bad. I just told them to screw off; they weren't the ones who were hit.

As we went through the month of January, I started driving one of the second platoon tracks. Ben McGeachey and Johnny Farley taught me everything that I needed to know about driving and maintaining the track. I learned how to replace track pads, boogie wheels, and various other things necessary to keep the track ready to go at all times. Months later, I would find myself very grateful to both of them for their guidance. Along with driving track, I also continued to go out on ambush patrols, and various activities around the village of AnDien.

Driving track was a job that got passed around a lot. When things were kinda slack, it seemed like everybody wanted to drive so they could dodge the dismounted operations. Then one of our tracks would hit a mine, and another driver went home without his right leg below the knee. Still being a relatively new guy with just three months in-country, whenever the old guys decided that they didn't want to risk losing a leg, the job got passed back down to me or one of the other newer guys.

I drove the second squad, second platoon track for about two months, and then I drove for two different Company Commanders for around five months. Through the grace of God, I never hit a mine.

1st platoon, Charlie Company, 1st of the 16th (mech).
(Photo courtesy of Jerry Hartman.)

2nd platoon guys, with the spoils of war. From back left: Don Brouwer,
Greg Goldenstein, Mike Nelson, and Mike Renshaw.
Left front: unknown.
(Photo courtesy of Mike Nelson.)

Jerry Hartman's track after it hit a mine.
(Photo courtesy of David Jeffrey.)

Monsoon season.
(Photo courtesy of David Jeffrey.)

Front row: Mike Nelson, Lt. John McCarthy. Standing: Ron Mackedanz
on the left, Johnny Farley on the right. Others, unknown
(Courtesy of Mike Nelson.)

8

TET 1969—VIETNAMESE NEW YEAR

DURING NOVEMBER 1968, CAPTAIN WENDELIN Winslow, who had been the Company Commander of the Bandidos when they came up to the 1st Division from the 9th Division in September, 1968, was replaced by Captain Sherwood "Woody" Goldberg. Captain Goldberg would command the Bandidos during the time of the expected Tet offensive and on through March, 1969.

While under his command, the second platoon operated pretty much on its own near the village of AnDien. The remaining platoons, headquartered out of FSB Huertgen, operated in the Iron Triangle, the Hobo Woods, and a couple of villages southwest of Lai Khe. Along with attempting to win the hearts and minds of the local peasant population, they also guarded the Army engineers who drove Rome plows, knocking down trees and other vegetation that the VC and the NVA would use for cover as they attempted to move into position to strike against the U.S. troops and the South Vietnamese soldiers.

Much of this same area was heavily doused with Agent Orange, which defoliated everything in the area. To this day, many of the men who served with the 1st of the 16th and other units of the 1st Infantry Division continue to suffer the results of the dreaded chemical defoliant. It has taken the U.S. Government years to finally concede that this chemical is tied in to such maladies as Type 2 diabetes, skin rashes, heart disease, prostate cancer, brain tumors, birth defects in children of veterans, and so on.

Medics from the 1st Bn, 16th Inf. (mech) providing medical services to
the village of AnDien, January, 1969.
(Photo from th author's collection.)

During the last two weeks of January 1969, we were all on
edge, expecting the worst. That being an all-out effort by the Viet
Cong and the NVA to show the Americans that they were still capable of creating a ruckus. As things turned out, the enemy had
not been able to build back up to strength to do any real damage.
They continued planting land mines, booby traps, harassing the
local peasants, and otherwise just being a general pain in the butt.

The month of February 1969 is difficult for me to recall.
From what First Sergeant Al Herrera has told me, the second platoon rejoined the rest of the Company and we operated in the
Michelin rubber plantation and the Iron Triangle during that
time. I had taken over the duties of driving one of the second platoon tracks. Due to attrition, moving into this position was inevitable. By now, having been in country for four months, and
with lots of newbies coming in behind us, I could either take on
the task of being a squad leader, a track driver, or a fifty
gunner/track commander. Having made the conscious decision
in basic training to be responsible for as few people as possible,

Ron Mackedanz with kids from AnDien.
(Photo from the author's collection.)

I chose to drive. The benefits of driving were that I stayed with the track most of the time. Along with the fifty gunner, I remained ready to react to any situation that my squad might happen upon. If they got into some heavy contact, I had to get to them and bring in the big guns.

The downside of driving an APC in 'Nam was that as the driver, I was the only member of the squad who actually rode inside the track. Everyone else rode on top of the APC. If we hit a mine, the driver was the guy most likely to be injured or killed. Many of our drivers went home with their right leg missing below the knee. Most drivers placed sand bags (about six layers) on the floor of the drivers hatch to help protect them against mines. However, due to the fact that the accelerator was on the floor, the right foot and leg were virtually unprotected. If we were unfortunate enough to hit a mine with the driver's side track, kaboom! Very few drivers survived that without some kind of injury. Depending on the size of the mine, the damage could be minor, such as having a track blown off, or some boogie wheels damaged. Frequently, the VC would place these mines on rice paddy dikes, where they figured we'd be crossing with a column of tracks. Most often they were placed on roadways and trails through the rubber trees or jungle. Knowing full well that the Americans were creatures of habit, eventually someone would take the easy route, and then there would be hell to pay.

During our time in the Iron Triangle, we had some tanks (from Bravo Company, 2nd of the 34th) assigned to us. These bad boys were nice to have around when we needed their fire power, but they had trouble negotiating the rubber plantations. The trees were planted far enough apart for the APCs to get between them, but the tanks were of little use in the rubber plantations and rice paddies.

One day, after one of the tanks was disabled, a tank retriever was sent out to FSB Huertgen to take it back to Lai Khe for repairs. The second platoon was going about their jobs, providing medical assistance and security for the people of AnDien, when the tank was pulled down through the village. Just north of the village was about a mile of wide open rice paddies, and then the Thi Tinh River Bridge crossing into the provincial capital of Ben Cat. Needless to say, this bridge was not rated for the tonnage that was about to cross it, but it was the only bridge to get across the river. With the tank in tow, the tank retriever started across the bridge. Once the tank was on the bridge, along with the tank retriever, the bridge started to shake and jump. Then down she went, with the tank and tank retriever sitting squarely in the middle. Luckily the river was not very deep at that time of year, and both vehicles and crews were recovered. With the exceptions of the major butt chewings that were administered at various levels, there were no injuries.

The following is Captain Goldberg's first-hand account of the happenings of that day.

Ah yes! The infamous bridge at AnDien, South Vietnam! The mission for my mechanized infantry company was counterinsurgency, win the hearts and minds of the local villagers, and we became one, often drinking tea with the village elders. A new added mission, based on new intelligence, was to defend the bridge across the Thi Tinh River next to the village of Ben Cat, from a reported attempt by the Viet Cong to blow it up.

This was no problem, except the Jewish Chaplain from Saigon came a-calling that day. With that came corn beef sandwiches and bagels and all that good Jewish food. With the food came a brief bible lesson and a prayer. There weren't many Jewish Chaplains in Vietnam, so this was a big deal for the three of us in my mechanized infantry company as we gathered on my bunker, fully engrossed in the words of wisdom that were being imparted by the rabbi.

As fate would have it, out of the corner of my eye, I spied a tank retriever towing an M-48 tank, hell bent, coming down the road towards my bridge. You guessed it, when they got in the middle of the bridge, the weight collapsed the bridge. Bingo! There goes one officer's career down the river.

As often was the case when things were not as you might want them for a VIP guest, the Brigade Commander, Colonel Robert Haldane, swooped down out of nowhere in his helicopter. I excused myself from the rabbi, and sharply reported to the Colonel, under the blades of his helicopter. He asked, "How goes it Goldberg?" My reply was, "Fine sir! Welcome to Bandido Charlie 1st of the 16th of the Big Red One. And about the bridge, we will have a temporary one up in no time." The colonel smiled in a "You have to be kidding me" way. "But sir," I said to change the subject, "I would like you to meet my rabbi."

After a very brief social talk, I did my thing. I turned to the colonel and said, "I have a favor to ask, sir." The colonel exclaimed, "A favor at this time, after what just happened?"

"But Sir, the rabbi has services tonight back in Saigon. See, it is our Sabbath tonight and he is caught on this side of the

The collapsed bridge at AnDien.
(Photo courtesy of Al Herrara.)

river. Might I borrow your chopper to get him back to Saigon before sundown? What saith the good Colonel," a West Pointer 1947.

"Goldberg! What do you Jews call it, chutzbah? I think you have chutzbah. Get him on the chopper and get it back to me as soon as possible. I do have a brigade to run and a war to fight." Off went the Chaplain and this one each Captain went to work on the new bridge. Lesson to be learned: With all due respect to the clergy, keep focus on the mission and pray later, after the fact.

Believe me, senior officers somehow never forget us when we goof. To this day, I guess the bridge matter did leave an impression. That colonel, who became a three-star, never missed the opportunity over the years to retell the story whenever I was present. And he always laughed about it! Even in war there is some levity, it can be said.

Shortly after Bandido Charlie Company moved out of the Iron Triangle, we received a report that the company that replaced us (Bravo Company 1st of the 16th mech) had been out on a routine patrol through the rubber plantations. The VC had buried a 500-pound bomb that had been dropped by our Air Force. Unfortunately, from time to time some of these bombs didn't explode on impact. The VC would dig a hole and bury the bomb, placing a pressure detonator or some other trigger device on the bomb. As luck would have it, the Bandidos had not come across this particular bomb. Bravo Company would not be so fortunate. The unconfirmed report we got was that, while out on a routine patrol, one of their tracks had hit a mine, which turned out to be that 500-pounder. The track was totally destroyed, and the six guys on the track were blown to pieces. For what it's worth, they never suffered.

When we left AnDien and the Iron Triangle, we went north on Highway 13 to the Michelin rubber plantation. We operated up there for a couple of weeks, doing recon in force and search and destroy missions. Our job was to seek out the enemy base camps and supply routes and destroy them, killing or capturing any VC or NVA that we encountered.

After a few weeks, we were assigned Rome plow security. As I recall, we operated southwest of Lai Khe in an area known as the Hobo Woods. Our main base of operations was FSB Mons. The job of the Rome plows was to knock down the triple canopy jungle that the VC and NVA were using to conceal their supply routes and base camps. The guys running these huge plows would quite often hit mines with the blades of the plow. Usually, due to the huge weight of the plow, there was very little damage. The driver would get his bell rung and might get shook up a little, but I can't remember ever having to dust-off any of them.

Whenever something happened, a couple of squads would dismount from the tracks and move in to cover the disabled Rome plow and protect the driver. Then one of the other Rome plows would hook up and pull the disabled plow out to where they could work on it. These guys could fix anything, anytime, anywhere. Usually within a few hours, they had the disabled plow going again.

On several occasions while we were at FSB Mons, we were hit by VC mortar and ground attacks. One night as we were under attack, I was watching some helicopter gunships working the perimeter just outside of the wire. They were pretty low as they worked over the enemy positions. All of a sudden, an RPG fired by the VC narrowly missed one of the gunships. After that, they sought the safety of the higher elevations. During March 1969, the Bandidos lost another man, killed on March 24, 1969, Sergeant Allen R. Miller. One other Bandido, Robert Metlock, was severely wounded by the same mortar round that killed Miller. It was Metlock's sixth Purple Heart. He is alive and well, living out in Washington.

Around the first week in April 1969, Captain Sherwood "Woody" Goldberg turned over command of the Bandidos to a friend of his, an Armor officer named Captain Kenneth Costich II. As a guy who, up until that point, spent all of his time in the second platoon, I must admit that we really didn't pay much attention to who the Company Commander was. We hardly even knew the man. Unless you were one of his crew or a platoon leader or platoon sergeant, you took your orders from your chain of command.

Little did I know, that was about to change. Captain Costich told his First Sergeant, Alfredo Herrera, and his Executive Officer, 1st Lt. Robert Barouski, to find him a new driver. For reasons that are still a mystery to me, I was chosen as the driver for the "Old Man." This was considered by some to be a soft job, but that depended on the Commanding Officer. With Captain Costich taking command, he kept us out in the action, which is where I would have been with the platoon anyway.

I must admit, I did miss the guys from the second platoon, but I still hung out with them whenever we were back in the fire support bases and night defensive perimeters. Mike Nelson, Greg Goldenstein, and Norm Hardin were a few of the guys that I remember hanging out with the most. Nels and Goldie were both from Minnesota, so it was like we were the three Minnesota Musketeers. Nels, from Caledonia, and I got to Vietnam about the same time. Goldie, from Fifty Lakes, got there about a month after us. Norm "Corky" Hardin was from Burton, Michigan. The camaraderie of these guys helped to keep spirits from dropping in the crapper. Many good times were had, even though we were living in hell.

Other guys that I got to know pretty well were David Komes from South Dakota, Ed Emmons from Maine, Mike Renshaw from New York, Al Kalchik from Michigan, and Chuck Richards from New Hampshire. Unfortunately, Chuck Richards passed away in September 2006. Our former 1st Sergeant, Al Herrera, Mike Renshaw, and I went out to New Hampshire in May 2007 for a memorial for Chuck. His sons, Matt and Josh, along with other family members and friends, were there to share stories and remembrances of Chuck.

Matt and Josh Richards, Al Herrera, Ron Mackedanz and Mike Renshaw, at the memorial for Chuck Richards, May 2007.
(Photo from the author's collection.)

Chuck Richards manning the fifty.
(Photo courtesy of David Jeffrey.)

9

TIMES—THEY ARE A-CHANGING

ARCH 1969 WAS TO BRING many changes. The second platoon of Bandido Charlie Company was back with the rest of the Company and moving north into the Michelin Rubber plantation. My recollection of this is very limited. From talking with my former 1st Sergeant, Al Herrera, he mentions that we were up there for a couple of weeks.

After that, we went back down southwest of Lai Khe, to FSB Mons. Here, we operated with Rome plows. Each day the platoons would go out and provide security for the engineers who were running and maintaining the big Rome plows. I remember thinking that as bad as the infantry could be from time to time, that I would rather be infantry than driving one of those. Those guys were literally sitting ducks on those plows: not just for the VC snipers, but for the snakes, fire ants, and other creepy crawly little critters that would fall from the trees they were knocking down. The mines and booby traps that they were frequently setting off were enough to keep us on edge twenty-four/seven.

When we finished up in the Hobo Woods, we got orders to escort the engineers and their equipment up north of Phouc Vinh. There, Alpha and Charlie Companies, 1st of the 16th (mech), would once again be providing security for the Rome plows. This time, our mission was to clear the triple canopy jungle from both sides of the road between Phouc Vinh and Song Be. This operation involved conducting search and destroy missions, mounted and dismounted ambushes, and building several new base camps as we proceeded up the road to Song Be. These base camps were named the Remagens. I distinctly remember being at Remagen 10 ,11, 12, 13, and 14. Charlie Company would occupy one base camp and Alpha would occupy another. Once the road was cleared five miles or so ahead, we would leap frog the trailing company ahead and establish a new FSB. Our Battalion Commander, Lieutenant Colonel Kenneth Cassels, and his staff usually accompanied the Company that was in the lead.

One day, Captain Costich came back from a briefing and told us that we were going up toward Nui Ba Ra mountain, looking for what the VC and NVA called their Victory Gardens. This was a real number ten (bad) assignment. No allied troops had been in this area since before the U.S. troop build-up in 1965. Accompanied by three or four tanks, we worked our way up the mountain and finally came upon several gardens containing peanuts and all kinds of other vegetables.

Our assignment was to destroy and disrupt the enemy supply lines, so we ran our APCs and tanks through them, pretty much tearing everything up.

We ran into some sporadic contact with the VC, but nothing heavy. One of the tanks got stuck in a low area, and it took several hours to finally get it out. During this time, Captain Costich walked back to Lieutenant Colonel Cassel's track to give him a situation report on the stuck tank. As he was making his way back to our command track, all hell broke loose. Enemy fire from the hillside was intense. Captain Costich, realizing that he needed to get back to his track, ran through a hail of bullets to get back and take command of the situation. He instructed Lieutenant De'Oliva and his platoon to take up a position flanking the incoming fire. Shortly thereafter, the enemy broke contact and disappeared. We were all happy to leave that area before darkness set in. There was a feeling in the air that nothing good would come from spending the night in this enemy stronghold.

A couple of weeks later, we were making our daily run from Remagen 12 to Remagen 13. Each day Lt. Col. Cassels would have his Company Commanders and staff officers gather at his location for a briefing. I always said that they were just having their daily tea and crumpets.

Each day, when not out on some operation, Captain Costich would take his command track, with me driving, along with three others, and we would head up the road to Battalion HQ. Quite frequently, we were accompanied by the Band-Aid track and two platoon tracks and their squads.

One particular afternoon, as we waited anxiously to get on our way back to our base camp, darkness was quickly approaching. Not wanting to be running the dangerous mountain road after dark, we were wanting to get going as soon as possible.

When the officers were finally dismissed, we saddled up and headed out. We had two tracks from the first platoon with us. One of them was in the lead. The other was running tail gun at the rear of our short column. Band-Aid track with Norm Hardin (from Burton, Michigan) driving ran second, and the Command track was running third. For some reason, the radio on the lead track was cutting out and they were getting out ahead of the rest of the column.

We got them reined in once or twice, but the third time they got out ahead left Norm Hardin basically running point. Shortly after crossing a small creek at a turn in the road, we started up a steep portion of the road. On the left side of the road, the terrain went almost straight up and was still covered by heavy jungle. On the right, the slope was somewhat more gentle and had been worked over by the Rome plows. As we were rolling up the hill, all of a sudden a rocket-propelled grenade was fired at and hit the last track in our column. The track swerved off the road and flipped over, throwing everyone off. As we were trained, Norm and I instinctively herringboned our tracks (one facing left and one facing right). At that point, we opened up with everything we had. Captain Costich called for artillery illumination rounds to light up our area. The artillery commander refused the mission due to the fact that we had friendlies in the area. Once Captain Costich was able to convince him that we were "the blankidy-blank friendlies," we got our lume rounds. Then with reinforcements coming from Alpha Company, we gathered up our wounded and headed for home. The crew on our lead track was there, wondering what all the commotion was about.

It appeared to me that the ambush was just a one-shot RPG, probably fired by a VC who crawled back into his spider hole and gloated as we expended many rounds of fifty-caliber machine gun and other small arms ammo on his behalf. In his effort, he had destroyed one Armed Personnel Carrier and wounded two American soldiers: one guy with a broken leg and one with shrapnel wounds.

Years later, in 1983, a small number of us "Old Bandidos" got together for a mini-reunion in Anderson, Indiana. There were four or five of us who had been in that ambush. Funny how each of us remembered the incident just a little differently.

During this time, we also came into contact with some of the local indigenous people called Montagnards. They were very primitive compared to the South Vietnamese people. They hunted with primitive crossbows and were very protective of their women. The word was that any GI caught messing with one of their women would die a very painful, excruciating death. To my knowledge, none of our guys ever took the dare to find out. There were plenty of local Vietnamese girls out plying their trade along the road to meet the needs of any of the guys who needed what they had to offer.

April and May were spent, for the most part, on the road to Song Be. All this time, I kept waiting anxiously for my R & R to Hawaii. Due to the high number of married guys in our unit, allocations for Hawaii were hard to come by. After being passed over again for the June allocations to Hawaii, I asked Captain Costich for an in-country pass so that I could go up to Da Nang and see my wife's brother, Mike. He was with a National Guard supply and support unit out of Winthrop, Minnesota, that got activated just a month or so before I got drafted. They arrived in 'Nam sometime in September, 1968.

When I got up to Da Nang, I found my way over to Mike's unit and went to the building where he worked as a finance clerk. It was around two o'clock in the afternoon on a Friday. There were very few people around. I asked a sergeant if Mike Wangerin was around. He told me to check down by the beach. Sure enough, he and his buddies were down by the South China Sea, working on their tans. When I showed up with my cleanest pair of well-worn jungle fatigues, they all looked at me like I'd just come from another planet. Evidently, nobody told them that there actually was a war going on in some parts of Vietnam.

We found a pair of swim trunks for me, and we spent the rest of the afternoon enjoying a little piece of Vietnam that until now, I didn't even dream existed. After a hot meal, we went over to the EM (enlisted men's) Club and watched and listened to a

My wife's brother, Mike Wangerin and some of the guys from his
Winthrop, MN National Guard unit.
Rough duty, but hey! Somebody had to do it.
(Photo from the author's collection.)

Vietnamese band with a couple of scantily clad girl singers murdering popular songs of the day, such as "Rolling on the River." Their talents at singing were tolerated by a bunch of sex-starved GIs who were just happy to have some leg to look at.

After eight months in Vietnam, I finally found out who's been eating my steak. We certainly never enjoyed food like this out in the field. Second from the left, my wife's brother, Mike Wangerin, then Ron Mackedanz. No idea where the civvies came from.
(Photo from the author's collection.)

On Saturday, Mike's outfit had a big steak fry and beer bust. I remember several brand new galvanized garbage cans filled with beer and soft drinks chilling in lots of ice. After almost eight months of C-Rations and darn few hot meals, this was a real treat. I couldn't believe that some guys had to suffer so much like this during their tour in 'Nam. After filling our bellies with steak and all the trimmings, we all grabbed a cold beverage and went into a nearby building to watch some movies. It turned out they had some little Korean guy with some really bad skin flicks. After watching some of these very poor flicks, I thought that some of the guys were going to kill the old guy. He was lucky to get out of there with his hide.

The following morning I had to catch a flight back to Lai Khe. After sleeping in a bunk with clean sheets and a fan blowing over me for two nights, I came down with a lousy cold. Kinda funny; I had been sleeping out in the rain and chilly nights for the past eight months and never had a cold, but two nights of comfort, and Bang! I fought that cold for two weeks. The good life of a rear echelon soldier was not to be for me. As things turned out, Mike's unit got an early out, and they were back in "the world" some time around the first week in August.

Shortly after I got back out in the field, our task of clearing the jungle from the road to Song Be was nearing an end. Our last base camp, FSB Remagen 15, was just outside of Song Be. The red clay soil and the monsoon rains made this FSB a real mud hole. We loaded the Rome plows up on low boy trucks and escorted them back down Highway 1-A to Di An.

Second platoon Bandidos, waiting for the Rome plows to load up for
the move south. Seated: Don Lane. Far right: Sgt. Ed Lester. Third from
right: Mike Renshaw. Others unknown.
(Photo from the author's collection.)

10

NO MORE ROME PLOWS

AFTER SEVERAL MONTHS OF PROVIDING security for the engineers operating the Rome plows, we were back doing our main job as mechanized infantry, making mounted and dismounted recons, search and destroy missions, nightly ambush patrols, and so on. We operated out of a couple of FSBs south and east of Lai Khe for a couple of weeks. Toward the end of June, Captain Costich was due to turn over his command of Bandido Charlie to a new Commanding Officer. As things would turn out, he got some kind of a stomach infection and left a couple of weeks earlier than planned.

We were back in Lai Khe for stand-down when the change of command took place, and Captain Phil Greenwell took over the company. Captain Costich left the company and I never heard of him until back in about 2003, when I came across his name on "Classmates.com." I e-mailed him with a simple message: "Hello Ken, this is Mack. I was your driver in 'Nam." His reply was, "Mack, it's been a long time." A friendship ensued that can only be shared by two people who have combat experiences together.

Phil was a young twenty-two-year-old captain. We didn't see too many of them. Most of the Company Commanders were between twenty-five and thirty-five years old with several years in the service. As things turned out, youth was no drawback for Phil. He took command, and we never missed a beat. We were operating out of a FSB called Bandit Hill in late June, early July.

Our Company HQ was set up in an old bombed-out building with a road running right through the middle of the camp.

During the day, some of our platoons would go out on dismounted patrols, looking for VC or NVA activity. Occasionally, we would go out in a company-size force on these operations. Several of these missions would last two or three days, during which we would just set up a night defensive perimeter (NDP) and send out LPs and a couple of ambush patrols. During this time, we were getting more and more *Hoi Chanhs* who became what we called Kit Carson scouts. They worked with us in locating VC tunnel complexes and weapons caches. There were a few we didn't trust one hundred percent and we were constantly on guard that they might be leading us into an ambush. However, during my time that we worked with them, that never happened.

One night, while we were operating south of Bandit Hill, we got into a small firefight with some VC. We captured a couple of them after they had been wounded. One of them, a woman, was like a wild cat caught in a trap. She fought the South Vietnamese (ARVN) soldiers who were taking her in, all the way. If she could have grabbed one of their weapons, she would have fought to the death. The last I saw of her, they (the ARVNs) were taking her away for interrogation. It was not a pretty sight. The Vietnamese soldiers on either side were not very forgiving of prisoners who didn't cooperate.

Back at FSB Bandit Hill, we were constantly beseeched by Vietnamese kids begging for anything that they could get their hands on. We had a garbage pit at the edge of our perimeter, and some of the kids would crawl thought the concertina wire and search through the garbage for anything that might be edible or otherwise useful. We had orders to keep them outside the wire. One young boy, about ten years old, consistently ignored our commands to *di di mau*. We would holler at him to get out of there. We would tell him, "*Di di*, or we will shoot your little ass." Of course, he knew that we were only bluffing.

Finally, after this had gone on for several days, one of our guys took an M-79 buckshot round and took the buckshot out of it. He then put the rubber cap back on the canister and loaded it in his thump gun. The next time that kid came around, it was followed by the usual threats, which he ignored until this guy leveled his thump gun on him. At that point, he started running for the wire. Just as he was hitting full stride, the rubber cap from the thump gun spanked him right on the hind end. His eyes got as big as saucers, and we never saw him back inside the wire after that. So much for winning the hearts and minds.

We were still at Bandit Hill when I received the news that my allocation for R & R had finally come through. My dates for Hawaii were July 11 through July 17. I wrote Janet a letter confirming this, and she got her plane ticket and was waiting for me when I got to Hawaii. After almost nine months of separation, we were really looking forward to spending some quality time together. When we got to Honolulu, they had the guys come into an area where all of the wives were standing, each one anxiously waiting for her man. I remember not even seeing Janet until they called out my name. Then she worked her way up to the front of the group of gals. I was starting to think that she hadn't made the flight over. I had forgotten that at four-feet-eleven, she was about a head shorter than most of the other women there. No matter, she looked really good to me when I first saw her again.

I had booked a room through the R & R services at the Ilakai Hotel on Wakiki Beach. We were in paradise. We went out to eat at some pretty fancy places, and one day we rented a convertible for a drive to the other side of the island of Oahu. We took in a few of the local sites, Diamond Head, Waikiki Beach, the Blow Hole, and a few other sites. But mostly we spent our time just being together, trying to make up for the past nine months.

All too soon, our time was over. I had to stand by and watch Janet board a plane back to Minnesota. The goodbyes were hell, not knowing if my last three months in 'Nam were going to be survivable. As her plane was sitting on the tarmac at the Honolulu airport, a few stragglers were boarding the plane as I stood there waiting for her to depart. One of the last passengers was a long-haired hippie type. As he got to the top of the stairs, just before he entered the plane, he dropped his pants and mooned his friends who were there to see him off. At the time, I wished that I had a rifle. I would have shot him right in his lilly white ass.

Later that day, I was on a plane heading back to Vietnam. Shortly after my return from Hawaii, our company moved from Bandit Hill to FSB Jim, the place where I started out in October of '68. From there we conducted the usual mechanized infantry operations, which often included being called to the rescue of some MACV (Military Assistance Command,Vietnam) or ARVN (Army of the Republic of Vietnam) unit. We had some artillery with us at FSB Jim this time around. The base camp had been enlarged considerably since October 1968.

One of the missions that we were sent out on was to engage some NVA in a base camp that had been located by one of the recon patrols. We were heading in toward the location of the base camp. As we were busting jungle with our tracks, all of a sudden I dropped the front end of our track into a bomb crater. Everybody on the top was thrown clear. The next thing that I knew, Captain Greenwell and most of the other guys were on another track continuing the assault. That left me and one other guy sitting out there with a useless fifty-caliber machine gun pointed down into the bomb crater. We found a spot a few yards away from the track and waited for the fleeing NVA to come running our way, fearing the worst.

As it turned out, the base camp was vacant when our guys got there. From the looks of things, the NVA had bid a hasty retreat, obviously not wanting to have anything to do with the firepower of Bandido Charlie. It wasn't long before a couple of tracks came back and pulled me out of the bomb crater. Then we proceeded on to catch up with the rest of the company. The NVA evidently decided that retreat was the finer point of valor for the day.

On another mission when we were out busting jungle, I hit a tree that had a nest of fire ants in it. Trust me; you have never seen a half dozen soldiers strip down so quickly, trying to get at the ants taking seemingly large chunks of their anatomy with every bite. Phil Greenwell swears to this day that I purposely knocked that nest of ants down just to initiate our new Company Commander. With the results of the ants chewing me up as well as everyone else, I doubt that was the case.

We were called one day to rescue the MACV group that was being overrun down south of Claymore corners. When the bad guys heard the Bandido Charlie tracks closing in on them, they broke contact and *di di'd*. On another search and destroy mission, we found a VC claymore mine factory. Unfortunately, we were a few klicks out of our AO (area of operation). When we called it in, the First Cavalry refused to authorize our encroachment into their AO. They were more than eager to take credit for finding the claymore factory.

Mike Nelson, Greg Goldenstein, and Norm Hardin playing poker. Goldies showing aces over eights. (Where the devil did the chairs come from?) (Photo courtesy of Mike Nelson.)

11

THE BATTLE OF BINH LONG PROVINCE

O N AUGUST 7, WE WERE notified that we would be heading up
Highway 13, also known as Thunder Road. We saddled up
at FSB Jim and headed balls to the walls up to the area around
An Loc. The 11th ACR (Armored Cavalry Regiment) was taking
part in Operation Kentucky Cougar and they needed a couple
of Mechanized Infantry Companies to assist them. Battalion
HQ, along with Alpha Company 1st of the 16th and Bandido
Charlie 1st of the 16th, were OPCONed (under the operational
control) to the 11th ACR. By 1530 hours, the 1st of the 16th
Iron Rangers had cleared FSB Jim and headed north. Our first
night up there, we later learned that we were set up in the middle of an old French mine field. Lucky for us, the old mines
were as competent as the French military during those years.
We arrived at FSB Aspen in the wee hours of the morning on
August 8.

The following morning, we made our way up to FSB Eagle
I and continued north to establish and secure FSB Eagle II. The
4th of the 9th ARVN HQ and a self-propelled 155 battery (six
tubes) were under our protection on this leg of the move. During
the next few days we operated out of several FSBs along Highway
13. On August 10, we received information that a company of
NVA soldiers out west of An Loc, in the area of (XT637972) near
the Fish Hook, wanted to *Hoi Chanh* (surrender). About twenty-
four guys from Bandido Charlie's second platoon were Eagle
flighted out on choppers to bring them in. Greg Goldenstein

(Fifty Lakes, Minnesota), Herb McHenry (Wadsworth, Ohio), and Don Lane (Shelbyville, Indiana), were on this mission, along with others.

Following is a first-hand account of that operation as told to me by Herb McHenry.

While under the operational control of the 11th ACR, the second platoon of Bandido Charlie Company received orders to prepare for an eagle flight. This was highly unusual due to the fact that we were a mechanized infantry unit. Don Lane and I both felt like we were on a suicide mission—sending a small platoon-sized element to take in an NVA Company who supposedly wanted to surrender. Led by a fairly new Second Lieutenant named George Perabo, we were inserted into a cold LZ near some rubber trees. As soon as we were on the ground, we moved toward the rubber trees and into some elephant grass. Once we were on the ground it became apparent that this was most likely a trap. I was Lt. Perabo's RTO that day, when I saw what looked to be NVA soldiers in the elephant grass, crawling toward our position. The platoon had spread out, leaving a few meters between each man and when it became apparent that this may be a trap, we started throwing fragmentation grenades at the advancing NVA who were now less than twenty meters away. During the fire fight that ensued, twenty-one NVA were killed and a few were captured. Pat DeLaurie was gut shot in the first few minutes and Don Lane slung him over his shoulder and got him to a dust-off chopper. DeLaurie was out of there less than thirty minutes after he was hit.

The second platoon put down a high volume of suppressing fire into the grass with our M-16s and a couple of M-60 machine guns. Lieutenant Colonel Cassels was flying overhead in an observation chopper and he eventually called in an ARVN unit to reinforce the second platoon. By the time the ARVN unit arrived, most of the firefight was over. The ARVNs moved in to take over the operation from the second platoon and the Bandidos, along with a couple of our prisoners, were extracted by choppers.

The following day, August 11, 1968, Alpha Company, 1st of the 16th, was inserted into the area to do a recon in force of the area. They found twenty-one dead NVA from the previous day's contact.

Of the captured NVA, a couple of them provided information about an impending plan to take the provincial capital of An Loc and then call a truce. With that card in their favor, the NVA then planned to call for negotiations at the Paris Peace talks. It was quite evident that the NVA were building up their troop strength around An Loc and Loc Ninh, just a few kilometers from the Cambodian border. The 272nd NVA Regiment, with attachments from the 273rd NVA Regiment, were involved with this operation. I never could understand how once the NVA and VC soldiers were captured or surrendered, they would sing like canaries, giving information on their former comrades. But in truth, a large number of VC and some NVA were forced into serving, so by giving up to the allied troops, they were basically breaking their bonds of forced service.

The afternoon of August 11, 1969, the Iron Rangers were ordered to move to a newly established fire support base that would become known as FSB Allons II (XT727968). That evening, Bandido Charlie Company, with Delta Company 5th of the 7th Cavalry attached, was ready to provide reaction force wherever needed. Just after midnight, in the early hours of August 12, Alpha Company, 1st of the 16th, was alerted that they were to prepare to move to Chanh Than to reinforce the 9th ARVN Command Post that was under attack. Shortly thereafter, the entire Battalion (less Bravo Company, 1st of the 16th) was alerted for possible deployment to FSB Aspen (XT 749801) and several other hot spots that were being hit, including Chan Tanh, An Loc, and FSB Thunder IV.

Within minutes after receiving that order and suspecting an imminent enemy attack, the Bandidos of Charlie Company 1st of the 16th at Allons II were ordered to dismount their APCs (with the exception of the drivers and fifty gunners) and to secure the perimeter. Around 0300 hours, things quieted down and all elements of the Iron Rangers returned to their normal alert status.

At daybreak, around 0600 hours on August 12, 1969, Charlie Company moved out of FSB Allons II, with Delta Company 5th Bn of the 7th Cavalry attached, headed south of FSB Eagle II where they hooked up with Alpha Company, 1st of the 16th (mech). Alpha Company was securing FSB Thunder IV, just northeast of An Loc. FSB Eagle II had been hit by the NVA during the night and Lt. Col. Kenneth Cassels (Salt Springs, Florida) was given the order to go after the NVA who had attacked FSB Eagle II during the night.

As we made our way west from An Loc, we traveled through a rubber plantation. A few miles in, we saw Vietnamese people working the rubber trees. Off to the right was an old French plantation mansion. A few hundred meters west, there were no more workers. That was usually a sign that something was amiss. With Alpha Company in the lead, we came up to a small creek that looked like a possible trap.

The AAR (after action report) indicates that Charlie Company was in the lead. As the driver for the Charlie Company Commander at that time, the AAR stands to be corrected. Alpha Company was in the lead with Lt. Col Cassels at this time moving up and falling in behind the lead platoon in Alpha Company.

After several minutes, Lt. Col. Cassels moved up in the column to see for himself what was taking so long. He then ordered them to proceed, and he took up a position in the column about four tracks back. After another kilometer or so, the lead track in the column was hit with an RPG (rocket propelled grenade) and a fifty-seven millimeter recoilless rifle round. The driver was killed, and the platoon leader was blown off of the track. With his driver dead, his track destroyed and on fire, the platoon leader was somewhat disoriented. Lt. Col. Cassels ordered him to mount another one of his tracks and to engage the enemy.

As Alpha Company pushed ahead, three or four NVA ran across the road between some of the tracks. The lead platoon of Charlie Company headed after them in hot pursuit. The leg troops from Delta 5th of the 7th dismounted and prepared for the fight. After a few minutes, Charlie Company was ordered to pull up on line to cover the right flank of Alpha Company, who was now involved in a heavy fire fight with a large, dug-in NVA force.

We assaulted the hill coming on line with Alpha Company and LTC Cassels and suddenly found ourselves right in the middle of a hornet's nest. The first thing I recall was that an RPG went right over my head. Somehow, it missed me and Captain Greenwell, who was sitting on top of the track and right behind me. By this time, we were fully engaged in the battle. Al Kalchik was on the fifty, firing everything he had at them. We were still closing on the dug-in positions of the NVA when all of a sudden my track wouldn't move. An RPG hit us right in the engine compartment. Al Kalchik, 1st Sergeant Alfredo Herrera (Beaverton, Oregon), and everybody else was blown off of the track. The CVC helmet that I was wearing for radio contact is what I believe saved my hearing. Sgt. Carroll Prosser, with Alpha Company, told me a while back that he was beside me on my right side. He said that when the RPG hit the Command track, that it lifted off the ground a foot or more. Carroll and I had been on the same plane heading for Hawaii just a few short weeks prior to this, and now we were in the fight of our lives.

At that point, instincts just took over and I went into survival mode. I just remember that the service door for the engine was blown out and hit my right shoulder as I sat in the driver's hatch. I grabbed my M-79 grenade launcher and started firing at any target that presented itself. There were enemy soldiers dug in just twenty yards or so in front of us. There were snipers in the trees; they were all over the place. The noise of the battle was horrendous. We had around forty tracks, all with fifty-caliber machine guns firing. This, along with all the small arms fire and the incoming enemy fire, was deafening.

Ironically, as the firefight ensued, I don't recall the sounds of the gunfire, or what was going on to my left and my right. It was many years later that I learned that this is a natural occurrence when a person is in this kind of a situation. It was like I was deaf to the noise and had tunnel vision—I was focused only on the enemy right in front of me.

I recall one of them getting up to run, and I leveled on him and put an M-79 round right in his back pocket. A number of years later, I was talking with Gerald O'Dell from Gadsen, Alabama. He was the gunner on the Band-Aid track on my left that day. He told me that he remembered seeing me do that. Up to that point, I thought that it was just between me and God.

After firing several rounds from my thump gun, I decided that I needed to get out of the direct line of fire. Fearing another RPG hit, I crawled up through the drivers hatch, completely exposing myself to enemy fire, and jumped down to the ground. I then ran to the back of the track where I found Al Kalchik and 1st Sgt. Al Herrera. Captain Greenwell was inside the track on the radios, trying to get some artillery and air support. By this time, the Battalion command track and both of the Company command tracks had been destroyed. In recent years, Al Kalchik has told me that he actually came up to the side of the track and told me to get out of there. I do not recall that, but I have no reason to question Al on this.

As the three of us were hunkered behind the track, a round came in and shrapnel hit both Kalchik and 1st Sgt. Herrera. I don't have any memory of being hit at that time. I just remember that 1st Sgt. Herrera was hit in the lower stomach area and that shrapnel had severed the artery in his right arm pit. He was savvy enough to jam his left thumb into the wound to stop the bleeding. This undoubtedly saved his life. Al Kalchik was hit in the right arm and leg. I took my knife and started cutting his pant leg off, making bandages to tie around his wounds. A medic finally made it over to us and took over caring for the wounded guys. Realizing that we had nobody up on our fifty, I went in through the back door of the track. That's when I first saw Captain Greenwell on the radios. I got up on the fifty and started firing at the enemy positions.

The barrel of the machine gun was burned out, and I could see the tracer rounds going out in six-foot circles. Not being a very opportune time to change out the barrel, I just kept putting out a volume of fire. I had just loaded another box of ammo in the fifty and slammed the action shut. The next thing I knew, I was dropping down inside the track. I remember telling Captain Greenwell, "I'm hit, I'm hit." He looked at me and said, "You're all right Mack, get out of here." He probably kept me from going into shock. I had been hit in the neck, right shoulder, right hand, and right side of my back. That RPG was fired at me with the intention of taking me off the fifty. Although it didn't make a direct hit, it did accomplish its mission. The actual blast hit in the rubber trees just above and behind me. Years later, when I was reunited with Phil Greenwell, he told me, "Mack, you looked like hell. I didn't think that you were going to make it." I'm sure glad he didn't tell me that at the time. I was pretty well covered with blood. Some of it was my own; some of it was Kalchik's and Top's.

When I bailed out of the track, a medic was just finishing up with Kalchik and Herrera. He bandaged up my hand and my neck. We then got a stretcher out of the track and prepared to get Kalchik and 1st Sgt. Herrera to a dust-off chopper. Melvin McElreath (Newnan, Georgia), two other guys, and I grabbed the stretcher, and with 1st Sgt. Herrera running along side, we started running down the hill toward 1st Sgt. Herrera's track, which was being used to haul the wounded out to an opening where the dust-off choppers could land.

As we were running, McElreath got shot just above his right hip. The bullet passed through and exited near his navel. He fell down right on top of Kalchik and I fell right along with him when the stretcher dropped. McElreath stood up and ripped his shirt off, yelling a few choice words at the NVA. We then grabbed the stretcher and started down the hill again.

Once we got to Top's track, number 007, we loaded the most critically wounded guys on first. I was hanging back, very hesitant about getting on the track. I figured that the enemy had us flanked and that we would never make it out to the dust-off site without getting hit. If we took an RPG with all the guys down inside the track, we'd all be killed. Top saw me holding back and said, "Mackedanz, get on this track, right now." Not one to disobey an order from my 1st Sergeant, I climbed aboard and we headed out.

We made it safely out to the dust-off site and got on the chopper. I don't recall a lot about the entire trip out or the chopper ride to the aid station. Years later, Top told me that he was getting weak from loss of blood. McElreath, although gut shot, picked Top up and placed him on the chopper.

We learned some time later that Top's track got hit on the way back in. Mesker Massey (Murphysboro, Illinois) was driving, Sergeant Burkhart was the track commander, and a guy named Hill was on the fifty. When they got hit, the fifty gunner froze up. Massey got shot up pretty bad, Burkhart managed to throw both of the two other guys back on the track, jumped in the drivers hatch, and cleared the kill zone. He reportedly received a Silver Star for his actions of that day. Norm Hardin and Gerald O'Dell were right behind them on the Band-Aid track.

We had quite a few guys wounded that day, including 2nd Lt. George Perabo, who was shot in the leg, and Greg Goldenstein who, even though he was shot through the arm, remained in the firefight, refusing to be medevaced out for treatment. Herb McHenry reportedly had second-degree burns on his legs from all of the hot fifty-caliber brass that kept landing in his lap. He stated that he fired over fifteen thousand rounds of fifty-caliber ammo before he ran out. He then grabbed an M-60 machine gun and continued firing over the top of the fifty-caliber.

Destroyed track from the Battle of Binh Long Province on August 12, 1969. The freshly-dug ground is where the NVA soldiers were dug in. (Photo courtesy of Norm (Corky) Hardin.)

My memory of the aid station was that it looked a lot like the aid stations on the TV show "M*A*S*H." They triaged us there, taking care of the most seriously wounded first. I was put on a chopper and sent down to the 12th Evac Hospital in Cu Chi. When I got there, they dug the shrapnel out of my neck, shoulder, and hand—most of it, anyway. I remember (and if I live to be one hundred I'll never forget) the sound of the scalpel cutting into my neck as the doctor went after a piece that laid within a quarter-inch of my jugular vein. They never gave me anything to deaden the area where they were cutting. I vaguely remember uttering a few obscenities, possibly questioning the pedigrees of the doctor and his staff. To this day, I still have small pieces of shrapnel coming through the skin on my back every so often.

From what I can recall, I was only at Cu Chi for a few days. While I was there, I asked one of the Donut Dollies (Red Cross volunteers) to pen a letter home to my wife for me. My writing hand was all bandaged up, and it was very difficult trying to hold a pen, much less actually trying to write with it. I just wanted Janet to know that I was going to be OK, even though I had been wounded for the second time. At some point shortly after I was wounded, my wife received my Purple Heart in the mail. Up until then, she hadn't even heard from me. This came as quite a shock to her, as she didn't know if I was dead or alive. A day or two later, she got my letter. In all honesty, I can't say if the Army just sent it to her, or if I told them to send it home when I was in the hospital at Cu Chi. Either way, it caused her a lot of unnecessary worry and duress.

Bandidos, making a sweep of the battlefield from the preceding day. Notice the two APCs that were combat lost, and the trim vane from one of them up in the trees. The track in the center of the picture is the Bandido Charlie Command track that I was driving. Although it was already destroyed, our guys put a box of C4 in it and blew it up, in an effort to make sure the NVA could not salvage anything from it. All that's left of it is level with the track treads.
(Photo courtesy of Norm (Corky) Hardin)

12

CAM RAHN BAY

CAM RAHN BAY IS LOCATED on the east coast of South Vietnam. It was a major port for our Navy and it was also one of our largest military installations in Vietnam. Some of the soldiers, sailors, and airmen first set foot in Vietnam when they got to Cam Rahn Bay. Other points for incoming Americans were Da Nang, Vung Tau, and Saigon, via Tan Son Nhut air base. Each of these areas were relatively safe for Americans, and very few of them were issued weapons, or even allowed to carry.

During my year in Vietnam, I was fortunate enough to see each of these cities. All, except Saigon, had beautiful white sand beaches, as nice as any that I had ever seen. I entered and left Vietnam through Tan Son Nhut. I went up to Da Nang for a couple days of in-country leave to visit my wife's brother, Mike Wangerin, in June 1969. I spent two weeks or so in Cam Rahn Bay during August and early September. And last but not least, I spent a few days toward the end of my tour in Vung Tau on a three-day pass with a few of my Bandido buddies: Mike Nelson, David Komes, and Ed Emmons. Ahh! But that's another chapter.

After being wounded for the second time and with less than sixty days to go on my time in Vietnam, I was hoping that they would send me home. As it turned out, my wounds were not life threatening or going to cause any loss of limb, etc. I was put on a plane and sent to Cam Rahn Bay. There was an Air Force-staffed hospital there, right on the South China Sea. What a beautiful place—white sand beaches, volleyball and basketball courts, and a virtual R & R center. Unfortunately, except for the guys with superficial wounds, we weren't able to take advantage of most of the recreation facilities that were available. The barracks that we stayed in were but a stone's throw away from the South China Sea. Between each set of barracks was a bunker, dug down about four feet deep and covered with a big piece of steel culvert. These were about twenty feet long and covered with several layers of sand bags. They were meant to be used by the wounded guys and the nurses in the event of a mortar attack. In reality, they were seen by many combat soldiers as death traps.

It was not very common, but on rare occasion, the Viet Cong would send in a few mortars from *sampans* out in the bay. Then a couple of sappers would sneak through the concertina wire surrounding the hospital grounds and throw satchel charges of explosives in the buildings and bunkers as they ran through the virtually unprotected area. One day a couple of us guys were just sitting around, talking with one of the Air Force nurses. She told us about how she and four or five other nurses, who all lived together in a trailer house near the hospital compound, were sitting around one night, talking. Suddenly the glass on one of their windows broke, and in came a satchel charge. They were sitting around the dining room table and were frozen in place by fear. Fortunately for them and for us wounded guys, the charge didn't go off. She said that she had never been so scared in her life.

During the time that I was convalescing at Cam Rahn Bay, we were hit with mortars and sappers twice. The second time, just prior to my getting sent back to my unit, we got hit around midnight. I didn't feel like diving into one of the bunkers and giving the sappers the opportunity to throw a satchel charge in on me, so another guy and I ran over to Supply. We tried to get them to give us weapons. They wouldn't give us any, so we ran down to the beach where the guard bunkers were. These were always manned by the new guys, who we called Fanugies.

We got down there and found these two Fanugies and told them to give us their weapons and to not come back until it was all over with. They were so happy to get out of there, they ran for the cover of the main base. Sitting there in that bunker with a couple of M-14s and two clips of ammo, each with only eight rounds in them, didn't seem all that smart.

Believe me, this was no hero thing. It's just that after ten months in combat, we were not going down without a fight. As things turned out, no sappers made it through the wire that night, although there were several probes. A few mortar rounds landed within the hospital compound, one of them amongst a group of black soldiers who were sitting down by the basketball court, listening to their tunes on the radio. Several of them were wounded again, but I never heard how badly or if any of them were killed.

All in all, my stay at Cam Rahn Bay was not unlike my stay at Da Nang when I went up to see Janet's brother. I was still in a war zone, but things were pretty secure.

13

MARKING TIME IN LAI KHE

AFTER RECUPERATING FOR A FEW weeks at Cam Rahn Bay, I was sent back to my unit at Lai Khe. My hand was still not up to strength, so I was assigned various tasks around our company area. I did a little jeep driving, taking guys out to the airstrip to go on R & R or to get on the big silver "freedom bird" to head for home.

On my first night back to Lai Khe, I went to check out the sleeping arrangements. There were several GP medium Army tents set up in our company area for the enlisted men to sleep in. Each of these had a wood floor made up of artillery ammo boxes. They also had ammo boxes stacked five or six high, filled with dirt for protection from incoming 122-millimeter rockets sent courtesy of the VC and NVA.

There were no cots in any of the tents that were not claimed. I was dog tired, so I went to Supply and got a mattress which I threw down on the floor, and then promptly went to sleep. At some point during the night, I sensed something nearby. I looked down toward my feet in time to see a big brown rat come running up my leg and across my stomach and chest. It jumped off my left shoulder. About the time I realized what had just happened, here came another rat chasing the first one. Needless to say, I went directly to Supply, woke up the supply sergeant and got issued a cot. Getting up off the floor seemed like a capital idea, and I never had another visit from the rats. In my entire year in Vietnam, I do not remember ever seeing any cats. We used to joke about the fact that the rats were so big, the cats had all *di di mau'd*.

One of the guys that I remember quite well was Albert "Oscar" Papa. He was a Hawaiian guy who had arrived in Vietnam when the Bandidos were still part of the 9th Division. He was in the second platoon when I got to 'Nam in October 1968. From what some of the other guys told me, Papa had several Purple Hearts. Having been wounded a number of times, looking at him, he looked like a guy that you didn't want to cross. In reality he was a damn good soldier, one that could be counted on through thick and thin. I don't recall if he extended in 'Nam in order to get out of the Army upon his arrival home or not, but I'm sure that his year was up before September 1969.

In any event, when it came time for him to catch a plane to Saigon, I was charged with driving him out to the airstrip. I can't say that we had been best buddies during our time in 'Nam, but I had a lot of respect for him. As we were sitting there waiting for his plane to come in, he reached into his duffle bag and pulled out a beautiful Buck knife with an eight-inch blade. It was in a black leather belt case. He was concerned about whether or not he would be able to get through customs with it. Then he asked me if I'd be interested in buying it for twenty dollars. I just happened to have a twenty on me, and I took him up on it. A month later when I flew back to the states, I took it with me, and had no problem with customs. I still have the knife.

When his plane came in, he turned to me, and with a tear in his eye, he said something about not wanting to leave his friends who were still out in the field. But it was time for him to go. He had done his part and given his full measure.

Another job that I was assigned was going down to 1st Division HQ at Di An to pick up new APCs. During the months of August and September, 1969 , Charlie Company combat lost over thirty APCs. Most were hit with RPGs or were blown up by land mines. Sometimes we would go down and pick up supplies from

Di An. You would be surprised at the multitude of tasks that they could find to keep a guy busy.

On one of my trips down to Di An, I went in to the enlisted men's club to have a Coke. By this time, tension was starting to run between some of the white soldiers and some of the black soldiers. This was a time of racial unrest back in the states, and it was carrying over to the war zone. Some of the black guys were feeling like they didn't belong there, and that this was Whiteys' war. Still, when the crap hit the fan in combat, color didn't seem to mean anything. We all bled the same color, and if anyone needed help, someone would put their life on the line to get to them. There are a lot of black soldiers out there that I can say that I am proud to have served with, some of whom are good friends of mine today.

Back to the EM club in Di An: When I went to enter, there was a guard at the door. When he saw my Buck knife on my belt, he told me that I would have to check it before I'd be allowed to enter. Evidently, there had been a number of fights there lately and they weren't allowing anything that would pass for a weapon. I did get it back when I left.

Toward the end of September, while down in Di An, I was told to report to the personnel sergeant. They were in the process of switching from service numbers over to Social Security numbers. They issued me a new set of dog tags with my SSN on them. Funny how they had a system that had worked well for many years, but some administrative guru obviously decided that it needed changing. Enlisted soldiers had service numbers that started with "RA" (for regular army) and draftees' service numbers started with "US."

There always seemed to be a little ribbing between the draftees and the guys who enlisted, but in reality we were all trained to do a job, and we did a damn good job of it. One of my commanding officers once told me that when the crap hit the fan, it was pretty much impossible to tell the draftees and the enlisted guys apart. They both did what was asked of them.

Shortly after getting back to Lai Khe, I was put in for Sergeant E-5. I went up before the boards a couple weeks later and received my promotion to Buck Sergeant. Although I never had the chance to serve out in the field as a squad leader, the promotion did have its benefits when I got back to Fort Carson for the last six months of my stint.

One day, as I was walking down through the Company area, the entire Company was in for a stand-down. The new 1st Sergeant stopped me and told me to get my equipment together, that I was going back out in the field. Now, I wasn't shirking the duty, but with two Purple Hearts and less than a month to go in country, I really wasn't all that excited about going back out in the field as a squad leader and looking for a third Purple Heart. About that time, Captain Greenwell came by and asked what was going on. I told him that Top had told me to get my stuff ready, that I was going back out in the field. Captain Greenwell, although short of people out in the field, turned to Top and told him, "Mack has done his time in the field, he stays in the rear." With the Company heading out for some real number ten area out around Nui Ba Din (the Black Virgin mountain), I was more than happy to finish out my time in Lai Khe.

During my last week or so in 'Nam, a few of us guys got in-country three-day passes. We were all getting short, we had very little time left in 'Nam. We made our way down to Vung Tau, to spend our time at the in-country R & R center. They had a large casino and bar down there, along with a beautiful white sand beach and plenty of female companionship for anyone wishing to partake.

I was sitting in the casino playing penny or nickel slots, when in walks LuWayne "Butch" Schuft. He was the guy from my hometown that I'd come in-country with. I hadn't seen him in almost a year. He had gone to the 2nd of the 2nd (Mech. Inf.), and I had gone to the 1st of the 16th (Mech. Inf.), both with the 1st Division out of Lai Khe. Our paths never crossed during our entire time in 'Nam until we got to Vung Tau.

Mike Nelson, David Komes, and Ed Emmons and I returned to Lai Khe with less than a week left in-country. Captain Greenwell has, in the past few years, jokingly accused me of going on leave without an authorized pass from him. I assured him that he had signed our passes for us. In hindsight, the Executive Officer (XO) may have signed it. All I know is that it was legit.

At Vung Tau R & R center: Dave Komes, Mike Nelson, Ron Mackedanz, Luwayne Schuft, Ron Rhoden. October, 1969.
(Photo from the author's collection.)

Vung Tau or bust.
Ron Mackedanz, Mike Nelson and David Komes. October 1969
(Photo from the author's collection.)

14

BACK TO "THE WORLD"

On October 11, 1969, I boarded the big silver bird in Saigon and started my journey back home. We flew from Vietnam to Japan, where we got off the plane for about an hour. All that I really remember about Japan is that it was cold. Compared to 'Nam with temps around 100 degrees, the forty-degree temps in Japan were very cold. When we left Japan, most of us figured that we would be landing in Anchorage, Alaska. To our surprise, we landed at Travis Air Base in California. As we went through out-processing, we were told that a steak dinner was waiting for us. Most of us, however, just wanted to get processed-out and get a flight home. We were cautioned not to wear our uniforms to the airport in San Francisco, due to the anti-war protesters. To this day, that still torques me off. At the time, I'm sure that most of us didn't give a hoot one way or the other.

I arrived back in Minnesota on October 13 and was met by my wife, Janet, my folks, my youngest sister, Cindi, and my two youngest brothers, Curt and Neal. They picked me up at the airport in Minneapolis, and we drove out to my folk's home near Spicer, Minnesota. Janet had been living with them for a couple of months.

The following morning, we woke up to three inches of snow on the ground. What a shocker, from 100 degrees and a combat zone to thirty degrees, snow, and nobody shooting at me. This would take some getting used to. While I was in 'Nam, my folks had moved to a rented farm site near Spicer. It was nice to be away from people for a while, getting used to "the world." I cautioned my wife about maintaining a distance when waking me. After having spent most of the past year in combat, my reflexes were spring loaded, and the last thing that I wanted to do was to hurt her or any other family members. Over the years, I was to learn that for some of us, that startle reflex never goes away.

I had thirty days of leave before I had to report to Fort Carson, Colorado. After having been through 'Nam, I was really not looking forward to spending six months in Colorado playing war games in the snow. The Army had a policy during that time: If someone left Vietnam with less than six months on their obligation, they could request and receive a discharge from active duty. I would have had to extend in Vietnam for thirty-three days in order to get down under that requirement. With two Purple Hearts, and my unit in heavy action, I felt that it wasn't worth the risk. Had I extended, I would have most likely ended up back out in the field. I had the uneasy feeling that I might not be so fortunate a third time.

During my leave in Minnesota, Janet and I had a mission. I had decided that if I survived Vietnam, I was going to buy a brand new 1969 Plymouth Road Runner convertible. Mike Nelson and I had been talking about buying new Road Runners when we got home. As things worked out, when I got home, I found that I did not have quite as much money saved up as what I thought. So I figured that I had better drop the Road Runner idea. We decided to try to find something a couple years old, like a 1967 Ford Fairlane or something similar.

As we were driving through the lot at Town and Country Chrysler in Willmar, there it was: a beautiful blue 1969 Road Runner convertible with a white top. Janet was driving and I told her to just keep going, we couldn't afford it. The next day we went back to look at it. It seemed like it was just calling out my name, tempting me to come and just take one little look. Yielding to temptation, we stopped and looked it over. It was pretty much set up the way that I would have ordered it with one exception.

It didn't have bucket seats. With that disappointment, we left. After talking it over that night, we decided that we could probably live with the bench seat. As I recall, the sticker price was something like $3,400. I figured that being it was getting close to winter, they might deal with me on it. Convertibles in Minnesota with winter coming were not a hot item on a dealer's lot. I really didn't want to pay more than $3,000 for it. That's what I could have gotten it for had I ordered it through the Post Exchange (PX) when I was still in 'Nam.

I thought that I had it all figured out. I was going to go with bank financing so I could get a cheaper interest rate and all that. On my third visit in to the dealer, I took my dad along. He had never bought a new car in his entire life. I thought that it would be a good experience for him and me. I dealt with a salesman who wouldn't budge on the price, so I looked at my dad, and then I stood up and walked out. Dad couldn't believe it. He knew how much I really wanted that car.

The following day, the dealer called me and offered to sell it for $3,200. I told him that I'd think it over and get back to him. A day or so later, Janet and I went in and signed the papers. Then I did something really stupid. The dealer said that they would take care of the bank financing for me, and like a fool, I let them handle it. As I recall, with their special financing arrangement, I ended up paying something like 12.5% interest. Our payments came to around seventy-five dollars a month. Man-oh-man, did I feel like the cock of the roost when we drove down Main Street of Willmar in that brand new Road Runner convertible.

In the fall of 1969, the weather was unusually warm. It wasn't long and we were out driving around with the top down, enjoying the new ride. Janet and I made a trip up to Fifty Lakes, to the home of Greg Goldenstein's folks. I had decided that I just might try to go deer hunting that fall, and Goldie had mentioned that I should come up and hunt around his area.

As things turned out, we were there right after Goldie got home. He and his brother, Bruce, told me of a couple places to

Plymouth Road Runner convertible, bought new in November 1969.
Sold in 1971 when gas went way up to fory-five cents per gallon.
(Photo from the author's collection.)

check out, and a week or so later, my brother Greg, my brother-in-law, and I were up there deer hunting.

I was a little bit hesitant about being out in the woods with a rifle, especially after having spent most of the last year in combat. We hunted an area north of Cross Lake that Goldie had told us about. After walking in a half mile or so, Greg decided that he was going to sit near a game trail that we had come upon. Mark and I headed west to check out a beaver dam area about a mile farther west. After still hunting our way through that area, we decided to head back toward Greg, as it was getting late in the day and we really didn't know the area all that well. We had just broken out of cedar swamp, when all of a sudden, "Bang! Bang! Bang!" I hit the ground and took cover, knocking Mark to the ground on my way down. I was very carefully trying to figure out where the shots had come from, when I heard Greg laughing.

Needless to say, I wasn't laughing. We walked up to him and took his gun away from him and put him up against a tree. I told him that if he ever pulled a stunt like that again, I'd kick his butt all over the woods. He apologized, saying that he just wanted to see how I'd react. To this day, he doesn't know how darn lucky he was that I didn't start shooting back.

After that little incident, and with temperatures in the seventies, it kind of put a damper on the deer hunting. As I recall, driving around with the top down on my convertible during deer hunting season just didn't feel quite right. So with the top down, and the sun in our faces, we headed south for Spicer. Suffice it to say that my first deer hunting experience after returning home from 'Nam didn't pan out quite the way I had hoped.

With the middle of November drawing near, Janet and I were making plans for our next six months in Colorado Springs. I would be spending my time there assigned to 1st of the 137th Infantry, HHC, 5th Bn. 10th Infantry, 4th Brigade, 5th U.S. Army. We loaded up the Road Runner with the things that we would need the most and headed for Colorado. Janet had a cousin who lived up around Littleton, and we had arranged for her to stay with them until I could find someplace off-post to rent. It wasn't long and I found a trailer park with a rental unit. I rented it and then I went up to Littleton to pick her up and brought her down to our new temporary home.

A lot of the trailers were being rented by other soldiers and their wives, so it wasn't very long before we got to know most of our neighbors. Right next to us lived an older couple (probably in their late forties) who became surrogate parents to a few of the couples down there. Harry and Dena were the caretakers of the park and they were great neighbors. Harry even tried to talk me into staying in Colorado and working with him on a very lucrative insurance repair business. However, thoughts of home and the lakes of Minnesota drew us back to the Land of 10,000 Lakes.

My assignment on Fort Carson was to a Communications squad in the headquarters company of the 1st of the 137th out by the old mule barns. As we were coming back from 'Nam, we were replacing Army Reserves who had been activated to hold down the post while the real soldiers were off fighting the war. (Let me be quick to mention, there is a lot of difference between the Reserves of today and the so-called Reserves of the sixties and seventies.) Very few units of the Reserves or the National Guard were activated for duty during those years, and those that were, seldom went overseas. My wife's brother, Michael Wangerin, was serving with a National Guard unit out of Winthrop, Minnesota, that actually went to 'Nam. They were a supply unit. They were activated in the spring of 1968, and they left for 'Nam in September, 1968. They got an early out, which brought them home around the first of August. I used to be a little bit envious of those guys, but today I wouldn't trade experiences with any of them for anything.

At Fort Carson, I did the best that I could to acclimate myself to garrison duty. Spit-shined boots, pressed fatigues, and all the other military bullshit was something that took some getting used to. I had a Hawaiian guy who was the commo sergeant and basically my boss. He was a Staff Sergeant E-6 with ten years in the Army. I was a Sergeant E-5 with eighteen months in the Army. He tried to tell me that I wasn't a real Sergeant because I had not been to Non-Commissioned Officer's school at Fort Riley, Kansas. I finally got tired of his crap and went toe to toe with him. I had a Combat Infantryman's Badge and two Purple Hearts. I told him, "Listen you S.O.B, I've been to the biggest NCO school in the world. Where have you ever been?" With ten years of service, he had never been outside of the States. After that, he never gave me any more crap.

We had a big general inspection one day. Like most units in the Army, we had a few items that we had either traded for or liberated from other units. Of course, these were unauthorized, and we would be reprimanded if they were found in the squad's possession. So the night before the GI, the commo sergeant loaded all of the unauthorized equipment, including an M-16 and other weapons, into his personal car and took them home with him, off post. If he had been stopped at the gate with all that stuff, he'd probably still be in Fort Leavenworth. As much as I didn't like the guy, the fleeting thought of calling the gate guards vanished. There are some things that you simply don't do, just to even some superficial score.

During one evening, Janet and I were out cruising Nevada Boulevard when a car pulled up along side of us and a guy hollered out, "Hey Minnesota! Where abouts you from?" I told him, Willmar. He then said, "Pull over," which I did, when I saw his Minnesota plates. Turned out it was a couple of 'Nam vets and their wives. The guy who asked us to pull over was Bruce Peters. He was from the Chokio/Alberta area up by Morris, and his wife, Clariss, was from down around Sacred Heart. Both towns are within an hour of Willmar. The other couple was from out in Wyoming.

During the next few months we became good friends and talked about getting together once we got back to Minnesota. Bruce had extended over in 'Nam, and he had a few more months to go before he could get out.

One day, as I was walking down through the Company area, I met another Sergeant with a SPC 4 who was being brought into the company. It was Chuck Richards, a guy from Bandido Charlie, over in 'Nam. I asked the other Sergeant what was up, and he told me that he was just taking Chuck up to sign in with our company. I asked him if I could handle it. He was more than happy to turn things over to me and disappear for the rest of the day.

Chuck and I continued up to HQ where we talked to the 1st Sergeant and he agreed to assign Chuck to my squad. Man, it was great to have someone from my old unit; it made time go a little faster.

Chuck, being an SPC 4, was required to live on-base, where I on the other hand, as a Sergeant, was allowed to live off-post. After a couple of weeks, Chuck bought himself a little dirt bike. I believe that it was a Yamaha 200 or something like that. On weekends, he and a couple other guys would get passes and ride out to Motor City. This was a place with several large car dealerships and some really big sand hills behind them. Janet and I would drive out and watch these guys for hours as they, along with dozens of others, tried to make it to the top. Quite a few of them wiped out before ever making it.

One Saturday, some guy came out with a Jeep and tried it. Needless to say, he got up there a good ways and stalled out. In an effort to back down the hill, the Jeep went sideways, and down the hill they came. As I recall, no one was seriously hurt, but the Jeep needed a little fixin'.

On occasion, as a sergeant, I was called upon to be the Sergeant of the Guard for our company area. The privates and SPC 4s would be out walking guard and every hour, they would report to the HQ where I would log it in. Things were getting a little sloppy, as we were not in any big danger of being infiltrated by VC or NVA, so some of the guys would make their rounds, report in, and then go to the barracks and crash for a half an hour or so. As things turned out, somebody broke into the mess hall and stole the eight-track tape player and radio. The next morning, Chuck was called in and questioned about the theft. I knew darn well that he had nothing to do with it, and that the only thing that he was guilty of was catching a nap while he was supposed to be walking guard. Either way it would have gotten him busted down to a private. The Criminal Investigation Department got involved, and they were looking for a fall guy. Things didn't look so good for Chuck. I wasn't going to let him take the fall for something that I knew was none of his doing, so I went down to CID and talked with them. The charges that they had pending against Chuck were dropped.

During the last six weeks of my time at Carson, the Army had come up with something that they called Project Transition. It was implemented to try to help soldiers ease back into civilian life. I signed up to work at the Post Exchange on Fort Carson, hoping to get into some type of management training. What a joke. I ended up working in the receiving department most of my time there. It beat playing Army, but not by much. There were a couple of older women who either were department heads (or just thought that they were in charge) who often referred to me as "the kid" or "hey boy." One day I finally got fed up enough and told them, "Boys don't come back from Vietnam." From then on, I heard a lot less of that kind of crap.

Around May 10, I started getting things together to ETS, otherwise known as getting out. I was afraid that I might be held over, due to a payroll error that had been made when I made Sergeant. However, the payroll department said that it was all taken care of. They signed my installation clearance record and after getting signatures on all the rest of it, on May 15, 1970, I was a free man again. Well, not really; I still had four years of Reserve time to do. This ended up being all inactive reserve time due to the fact that I had been in combat in 'Nam.

Janet and I packed up what we could in a U-Haul trailer, hooked it up to the Road Runner, and north to Minnesota we went.

PART TWO:
HOME AGAIN

15

FREE AT LAST

MAY 16, 1970, THE DAY that I thought would never come, was finally here. We were heading back to Minnesota, no clue as to what the future had in store for us. The job market had not improved since I had been drafted. We briefly considered the thought of going back out to California and picking up where we had left off. Somehow, after having spent some time out there, California had lost some of its luster.

Minnesota's draws, with its abundant hunting, fishing, and other outdoor activities, along with family ties, were strong. We decided that we would give Minnesota another shot. My folks were good enough to put us up for a while until we figured out what we were going to do. We arrived in Willmar with our new 1969 Plymouth Road Runner convertible, pulling a U-Haul trailer with all of our personal property in it. Some guy pulled up along side, smirking. I figured he thought that it was quite a sight—a muscle car, pulling a trailer. When the light turned green, I punched it and put him in my rear view mirror. Even with a trailer in tow, the Road Bird still had plenty of get up and go.

It seemed kind of weird to be out of the Army. Funny how I never gave much thought to the guys who were still over in 'Nam, fighting and dying. My war was over; at least that's what I kept trying to tell myself. I never talked freely with anyone about 'Nam, or the things that I had been involved with while serving my time over there. It seemed like it was best to just bury the memory, or try to anyway.

One of my uncles told me a few years back that I never wanted to talk about it. In some respects, I suppose that he was right. On the other hand, it seemed like no one wanted to hear about the horrors of war. No one wanted to believe that the things that happened in war were real, even though they were seeing it every day on the evening news: the carnage that was being brought upon our young soldiers and Marines on a daily basis. It was too easy to turn the TV to another channel and just go on with their lives as if the war had no effect on them. Unfortunately, after I got out of the service, I found it all too easy to do the same thing. Hell, my war was over. My job was done. I had fulfilled my obligation to my country and it was time for me to move on.

I spent the summer trying to find work. According to the Army, I was eligible to draw unemployment compensation for a few months. I went down to the employment office in Willmar and met with the local veteran's representative. He was typical of many WWII vets of the time. Most of them didn't accept the Vietnam vets as being real veterans. Vietnam, having never been a declared war, somehow made us less than honorable in their eyes. Many of the American Legion Clubs and the VFWs turned us away like we had the plague.

The veteran's representative at the employment office lined me up with a few low-paying, menial jobs, which would have actually paid less than the unemployment benefits that I was entitled to. When I told him that I wouldn't sweep up turkey guts at the local processing plant for $1.50 an hour, he stopped my benefits. He tried to tell me that I should use my military training in finding work. I told him that I thought that was a great idea, but I didn't think that the Mafia was hiring at that time. For some reason, he took a sudden dislike for me after that.

I did get a job driving a busload of young girls down to the seed corn fields around Olivia, where they worked de-tasseling seed corn. It was a job that employed many of the area youth during those times. Some crews were all girls and some were all boys. I can't imagine why they didn't want to get a bunch of fif-teen-year-old boys and girls together in a corn field. There may have been something other than de-tasseling corn taking place. I worked that job for a few weeks as a driver and field supervisor. After I fired a couple of girls who thought that they were out there for the sole purpose to beautify the place, I ending up get-ting fired because one of their daddies complained that I had used some profanity when I fired her. I guess the military jargon that I was used to just wasn't appropriate when explaining to a young girl that she wasn't needed on the job if she couldn't or wouldn't do the work. Oh well! Chalk that one up to experience.

I applied for entry into the junior college in Willmar. I wanted to take something along the lines of Business Adminis-tration. Due to the late date, and the fact that I had not taken my ACTs for entering college, I was rejected. The counselor told me that I might check with the vocational school next door. They did-n't have anything in business administration, but they had Mar-keting Management. I decided to apply and was accepted for the two-year course under the GI bill. It turned out that this was re-ally just a course in Sales and Marketing.

While I was waiting for school to start, I went to work for Duane Nelson and Sons. They built turkey barns throughout west central Minnesota. The first day of work, driving five-by-seven pole barn nails over my head, I thought that my arm was going to fall off. The crew was made up of Duane, his father, and his fa-ther-in-law (both in their fifties), and two or three of his teenage sons. We would meet at their place around five o'clock in the morning. Three or four guys would ride in the front of the pick-up truck (there were no extended cabs back then) and us young guys would ride in the back. Duane always seemed to have his foot on the floor boards. I know that we were doing seventy to eighty miles an hour most of the time. When we got to the job site, we worked our tails off. I don't remember what the pay was, but we earned every penny of it. Duane worked us hard, but he was right in there with us and never expected us to do anything that he wouldn't do. Even now, I run into Duane or one of his sons, and we talk about those days when I worked for them. Good people, all of them.

Janet and I stayed with my folks for the summer, and then we found a resort on Elkhorn Lake where we could rent the main house for the winter months. So, we made our first attempt at setting up housekeeping as civilians. The couple that owned the resort was nearing retirement and was scaling down the resort operation, so we had the place all to ourselves. The lake had good fishing for crappies and sunfish, which kept us somewhat entertained and fed.

16

THE GI BILL

ALL TOO SOON, THE TIME came to head off to school. When I finished high school, I never envisioned myself going on to college or anything. Hell, I had all I could do to get myself through my senior year in high school. My English teacher gave me a "D" just so that I would be able to graduate. English was not my favorite subject. She gave me a gift, and I have always been grateful to her for that. I always tell people that I graduated in the top ten percent of the bottom ten percent of my class. Probably closer to the truth than I care to think now.

The GI Bill provided an opportunity to further my education that I would have probably never been able to do without it. The state colleges and vocational schools were, at the time, tuition-free to veterans with an Honorable Discharge from the military. The Department of Veterans Affairs (GI bill) paid us around $225 a month to cover other school expenses and housing. This doesn't sound like much by today's standards, but back in 1970, it opened some doors for a large number of returning veterans.

It was quite an adjustment going back to school after having been out for four years. I was one of the older, non-traditional students. Most of the guys on the GI Bill were going to the junior college next door. Just a few of us vets were attending Vo-Tech, as we called it back then. Some of the vets started a Vets Club that met once a month in the upper story of the local Legion Club. I attended one meeting and was not very impressed. It seemed to me that all it was, was a big drinking party. Not being into that scene, I didn't see any reason to participate. Oddly enough, today some of those guys have been good friends of mine for around forty years. They learned to accept me in spite of my habit of being a non-drinker.

During my time at Vo-Tech, I got to be somewhat of an activist, which was quite a turnaround for me. I had always been somewhat shy and not all that eager to get involved in things that I didn't feel I needed to. The school faculty was full of doves and anti-war protesters. Some of them didn't seem too happy about having a combat veteran in their classes. If we could have been looked down on more, I don't know how. We sure never got the respect that previous veterans had received. I earned my keep, placing on the Dean's list with a 3.5 grade point average during my first year at Vo-Tech. It's funny how things changed when I was in school because I wanted to be there instead of having to be there.

At one point, the trial of Lieutenant William Calley came up. He was being tried for the murder of innocent Vietnamese peasants at My Lai. On March 16, 1968, right after the Tet Offensive, Lt. Calley and his platoon, having lost many of their men around the area of My Lai, started shooting up the village which most of their casualties were coming from. The end result was not pretty. Literally hundreds of villagers lay dead after their foray: men, women, children, old folks, anyone who moved. The Calley platoon had taken so many casualties from the village of My Lai that they didn't have a clue who was the enemy and who were the friendlies. Unfortunately, the Viet Cong would frequently use the peasants as human shields, or coerce kids into carrying a grenade or other explosive device in among a bunch of GIs and kill or maim anyone close by.

Often, the kids were threatened by the VC that their mother, father, or siblings would be killed if they did not do what they were told. After awhile, we got to the point where we didn't trust any of the Vietnamese. They all looked the same, and in some cases we got the impression that they would all just as soon see us dead.

Hauling the blown Pysops truck out of An Dien.
(Photo from the author's collection.)

At the time of the trial, I felt that Calley was being made a scapegoat and was taking the heat for officers higher up the chain of command. I was convinced to the point that I got a petition going and obtained over five hundred student and faculty signatures, recommending that Lt. Calley be acquitted of all charges against him. Today, I am not totally convinced that he and his men did in fact act out of frustration with the numbers of men that they were losing, and the fact that the VC were using the local population to hide behind. Certainly there is no excuse for the deeds done, but as a combat infantryman who has lost friends in war, I can somewhat relate to what they were feeling. Not being able to tell who was the enemy and who was not the enemy, all I know for sure is that they will have to make their peace with God, same as everyone else.

Back to school, we had classes in Introduction to Computers, which by today's standards are kind of archaic. Everything was done using the Binary code system. The computer filled a whole classroom and generated a lot of heat. It is still somewhat baffling to me how the computers of the early seventies eventually progressed into the tiny hand-held computers that we use today.

During my first year at Vo-Tech, we were introduced to marketing techniques, insurance, and basic English, math, and other pertinent subjects. The instructor that we had for the insurance class was Wayne Hoeck. He served in the U.S. Army Air Corps as a P-38 pilot. He was shot down over Germany, captured by the Germans, and held as a POW. He and another pilot escaped the prison camp and were picked up by a British tank unit. Like most WWII veterans, he never talked much about his service. In a recent conversation with his wife Joann, she told me that he never even told her about being shot down and taken prisoner until just shortly before he died in 2000. On rare occasions when we happened to run in to each other, he would share tidbits about his experiences. One of his favorite methods of story telling was to start out saying, "My brother told me . . ." Then he would go on about something that he had done, but was too modest to take credit for. Wayne Hoeck passed away a few years back, but I always remember him as a quiet hero of "the Big War." When he died, I felt like a lot of untold stories of WWII went to the grave with him. What a shame!

Lieutenant Wayne Hoeck, P-38 pilot during WWII. Instructor at Willmar Vo-Tech. (Photo courtesy of his family.)

I spent two years at Willmar Vo-Tech and received an Associate in Arts Degree in Marketing Management. Turns out that having that piece of paper allowed me to get a job as an assistant manager at a local department store making a whopping $2.25 an hour. WOW! I could have found something in the construction trades that would have paid over $3.50 an hour and not spent two years at Vo-Tech. However, in retrospect, they were two good years. I made quite a few friends who are still friends to this day, and we have had some great times together.

I went on to work for the Tempo department store for over two years. The best thing that happened while I worked there was that Janet and I had our first baby. Brenda Jean Mackedanz was born in October 1973, almost four years to the date when I got home from Vietnam.

When it appeared that the job at Tempo was going nowhere, I took a job in a small sporting goods store. That turned out to be a bad decision. The owner, Art Norby, was a great guy to work for, but he was in over his head. It's very difficult to compete with the established sporting goods stores in the area when you have limited capital resources available. I knew that things weren't going well by the limited inventory that we had and other tell-tale signs. Two weeks before Christmas, I took my paycheck to the bank and they refused to cash it. I went back to Art, and he went right to the cash register and covered my check right on the spot. The bad part of it was, he told me that he was closing up the store and I was unemployed. Two weeks until Christmas and a little daughter just one year old. "What a bummer."

I looked around for other work, and finally decided to take advantage of the two years of GI Bill that I still had available. Spring quarter was starting up in March and I figured that I could jump right in at that point. I had decided that I needed something to help that Marketing Degree, and accounting appeared to be a natural fit. The part that I had not considered was that I was coming in at a time when all the other students had already had two quarters of Accounting Principles and we were going right into

Cost Accounting. The instructor, Clarence Beiderstad, was a great teacher and a very knowledgeable person when it came to this subject. However, he was way over my head with my lack of Accounting Principles. He was not able to break it down to where I was able to comprehend what he was trying to get across. I washed out of his class in a matter of weeks.

This posed a problem with completing the Accounting curriculum on schedule with my fellow students. I got talking with some of the administration personnel about an Agricultural Business course. At the time, back in 1975, there was no such thing as an Ag Business course. I talked them into letting me take a couple of agriculture classes dealing with farm financing and such. This was more in line with what I was looking at. It turned out that by taking these classes rather than all accounting classes, it kept me from receiving a degree from the Accounting Department. I finished up my second year with a Degree of Occupational Proficiency. That was just a piece of paper which in effect said, "Sorry Charlie, you just wasted another year and a half and still don't have a college degree."

One of the really good things that happened, due in part to myself and one other accounting student working our way into the Ag curriculum, is that the administration saw the need for an Ag Business Program at the Vo-Tech, and one was started up the very next fall. It has been one of their most requested classes ever since it was instrumented in 1976. Without realizing it, we were spearheading a movement. Were we progressive or what?

The spring of 1976 found me finishing up with the accounting course, minus Cost Accounting. I had no job and baby number two was soon to make her appearance in our world. Being twenty-seven years old and in serious need of a job, I started my job search in earnest. We were told that if we could find a job paying seven thousand dollars a year, we had better jump at it. The school had a few leads that some of the students applied for, and they allowed us two school days to interview.

Knowing that I was not going to receive a full Accounting Degree, and with a baby on the way, I took a few extra days for job interviews. Our instructor and head of the Accounting Department didn't think very highly of my activities, but I figured that getting a job was more important than attending a few classes at the end of the school year.

I was following every lead that I could come up with. I wasn't going to sit back and expect the Vo-Tech to find a job for me. One day, I went in to Production Credit Association in Willmar. It turned out that the branch manager, Dale Baseman, was a school buddy of a couple of my older cousins from Hutchinson. He had just hired a guy as a loan officer that spring, but he mentioned that they might be looking for a loan officer down in Olivia, about thirty miles south of Willmar.

I went down there, interviewed, and about two weeks later, I had the job. It started out at eleven thousand dollars a year, company car, and full benefits. When I told the accounting program head about that, I thought she would be happy that one of her graduates was starting out with a good job and a higher pay rate than she had been expecting. Instead, she seemed PO'd that I had topped everyone else in my job search.

The day of graduation, my wife Janet said she thought that the day was here for our family to get bigger. So on that hot May evening while the class of 1976 from the Willmar Vo-Tech was receiving their degrees, I was at the hospital with my wife, witnessing the birth of our second little girl, Dawna Christy Mackedanz. WOW! That sure beat the heck out of an old graduation ceremony any day.

17

ON TOP OF THE WORLD

AHH! LIFE IS GOOD. NEW JOB, new baby girl, new home. With my new job working for Production Credit Association and everything looking up, what could be better? Shortly after starting work in Olivia, I found a farm house for rent, south of Danube. This put us about seven miles from where I worked. The farm place was owned by Brad Nere, a young farmer whose family had a dairy farm right across the road. Brad had a little boy with a gal that he was involved with, but he seldom, if ever, got to see the boy. As it turned out, our first daughter, Brenda, was about the same age as his little boy. Brad would take Brenda with him to the elevator in town and loved having her around. Needless to say, he spoiled her rotten. The entire Nere family was great. Our two years that we lived there were filled with good memories.

In 1978, Janet and I got the chance to purchase our first home in Olivia. The day that I had to tell Brad and his father, Leroy, that we were moving, was a sad day for all of us. Shortly after that, Brad got married and moved into the house.

My job with PCA involved writing loans to farmers for operating expenses and machinery purchases. This was new ground for me, but I quickly learned the task at hand. The farmers in Renville County, Minnesota, were the base of our customers. For many years, Renville County has been one of the most progressive agricultural counties in the upper-midwestern United States.

I worked for PCA in Olivia for eight years when I got the opportunity to transfer up to the Willmar office. So in 1984, we put our house up for sale and moved back to the area where most of our friends and family were. The branch manager at the Willmar office had left due to health issues, and this created the opening that I had hoped for for many years. We always wanted to get back up to the Willmar area and now the chance had come. We moved into a rental house in Kandiyohi for a year or so until that house was sold. Then about the same time that we were informed that we had to move, I lost my job with PCA. Funny how the bubble can burst. One day, I was on top of the world, and the next day I'm wondering what the hell happened.

I had worked for PCA for nine-and-a-half years; I thought that I was doing all the right things to secure my job: attending any classes that were offered to enhance my job skills, learning how to use the new IBM personal computers, et cetera. Evidently that wasn't enough. During the early eighties, the farm economy was going through some tough times. PCA decided to merge with Federal Land Bank. Due to this proposed merger, there were jobs that paralleled each other and someone was going to lose out. Well, I guess we know who that was. I was just six months shy of being fully vested in retirement, but they assured me that had nothing to do with my termination. Ya, okay!

Funny, how just weeks prior to that, I was working with a local poultry business, renewing their loan of several million dollars, and then I was out of a job. The loan was written for just a short period of time to cover their fiscal year end. The amount more than doubled the loan volume of our entire Willmar branch at the time. I worked with our PCA attorney, Robert Halvorson, to make sure that all of the i's were dotted and the t's were crossed, and met all of the requirements and no loop holes were to be found. Then he and I, along with my supervisor, who will remain unnamed, met with the entire board of directors for the poultry company. I laid everything out for them in a very professional manner, got the required signatures, and closed the loan.

They only wanted to use the money for a few days, but with the high risk that Farm Credit was taking, we made it a part of the loan agreement that they would hold the loan for two weeks. This allowed Farm Credit to collect more interest, thereby making the risk a bit more palatable. Shortly after the loan was closed, I was given my two weeks notice. One day the hero, the next day the goat. I was told that my job was being eliminated and, "We'll see you around." In reality, they hired a young gal fresh out of college, paid her half of what I was making, and all she knew how to say was, "Yup! Yup! Yup!" They didn't seem to realize that in just one afternoon, with my experience, I could make loan decisions that would save them that difference in pay. My supervisor had the audacity to ask me if I would be interested in working out of another PCA office, under a contract: No benefits, no lending authority, no guarantee of how long it would last, no promises, just doing him a big favor. The two guys who had worked out of that office had screwed things up and moved on to another office. I told him that I wasn't interested. I figured if they were firing me, why should I do anything to help them out?

I finished up my two weeks, during which time the poultry company repaid their loan in full, and I took my severance package and left. I went out and bought a new Ford Ranger pickup and took off for Wyoming to get away for a week to go deer hunting with some friends.

When I got back from my little trip, I went in to PCA and told them that I would take the contract out of the Benson office. I had given it a lot of thought, and realized that I had to do something to bring in some money and keep a roof over our heads, and put food on the table. I had to swallow my pride a bit, but we all do what we have to do when things turn bad.

The next several years were tough. The banking industry was not hiring any loan officers unless they had a college education. Ten years of experience without that diploma didn't mean squat.

Every place that I applied to told me that I was over-qualified for the position that they were looking to fill. It didn't take me long to figure out that overqualified was just a term for "we don't want to pay you for your experience."

At thirty-eight years old, I now found that I had several strikes against me in the job market. I didn't think that age would be one of them, but it seemed like every position that I applied for was being filled by young, inexperienced college graduates. The old days of employers looking for people who would stay for the long haul were over with. It seemed like most potential employers were hiring young people with the thought that they would use them for a few years and then replace them with younger people, thereby never having to pay a retirement plan.

It may have been just my perception of things at the time, but it appeared that every time a potential employer saw on my application that I was a Vietnam veteran, they immediately turned a cold shoulder to the interview. Many of them treated me like I was a potential bomb, just waiting to blow up, and "go postal."

There had been a few, and I say darn few, instances where a veteran had gone off the deep end and started shooting people. This of course, made all Vietnam veterans "dope-crazed baby killers, just waiting to go off." The public just couldn't see past the media B.S. and focus on the hundreds of thousands of Vietnam veterans who came back, got an education, a job, raised a family, and led a productive life with their family, attending church and paying their share of the taxes. The seventies and eighties were not good years to be a Vietnam veteran.

18

I'VE BEEN WORKING ON THE RAILROAD

I N 1989, I FOUND OUT that the Burlington Northern Railway in Willmar was hiring brakemen/switchmen. Although I wasn't all that interested in going to work on the railroad, I desperately needed a job. I went to the employment office and put my name on their hiring list. I had a couple of friends who worked on the railroad, and they seemed to be doing all right, so I figured "what the heck."

In December 1989, after attending about four weeks of training, both in the classroom and hands on, seventeen of us were hired on at the Willmar railroad yard. I signed on to work a yard job as a switchman. This job entailed working with three other guys or gals switching trains out, making up trains that would go from Willmar to Fargo, North Dakota; Sioux City, Iowa; Aberdeen, South Dakota; or Minneapolis, Minnesota. Most of my work was on the midnight shift. December 1989 was colder than a witch's broom handle. We would be out there working in below zero temps with the wind blowing off of the lake, trying to hook air hoses together that were stiff as a rail.

Working on the railroad with no seniority, we got called for all the crappiest jobs. We could forget about family birthdays or other special events. Christmas and other holidays were a thing of the past. We could bet that we'd be getting called to work about the time everyone was getting ready to sit down for dinner. If we were lucky, we got an hour notice, or call, as we knew it.

In 1985, the conductor's/brakeman's union voted away most of the rights for any new hires in exchange for productivity pay. This in effect gave each conductor, brakeman, and switchman who hired out prior to 1985 a productivity share for each shift they worked. At the end of the year, usually just before Christmas, they would get a big bonus (a productivity check of around ten thousand dollars or more) and the new hires would get what Johnny shot at and missed. That's the way our union brothers took care of us. The engineers, on the other hand, were so greedy that they sold away their rights to productivity shares for a one-time payment of two hundred dollars. Boy! Were they sharp or what?

I never was a big union man, but if I was going to work on the railroad in a union shop, I didn't have much of a choice. It always seemed like the company was paying me for the screwing they gave me; while on the other hand, I got to pay the union for the screwing that they gave me. What a deal!

New hires on the railroad received seventy-five percent of regular pay their first year. If they stayed with it, the pay increased by five percent each year until at five years we were up to what the "old hats" were making, less the productivity pay. But we got to do the majority of the work.

After working for one full year, BAM! Along came the first of the year in 1991. Without any notice, most of us that hired out in December 1989 or after were laid off. No job, no idea when we might get back on, nothing. Most of us hadn't been there long enough to draw railroad unemployment. So once again, I was sitting without a job. I worked whatever I could to make a go of things. Every once in a while the railroad would call me for a run to Fargo or Minneapolis. If I could catch a job at least once a month, it would keep our insurance going for the following month.

In June 1991, there was a new short line railroad that was starting up in west central Minnesota. The Twin City & Western Railroad was hiring about twenty-five people to run trains between Minneapolis and Milbank, South Dakota. They would be headquartered out of Glencoe, Minnesota. The training was being done at Breckenridge, Minnesota, in conjunction with the Red River Valley & Western Railroad. As we sat there on the first day we were hired, one of the big shots came in and told us that they had interviewed hundreds of applicants and that we were "the cream of the crop." As I looked around the room at what looked to be lopsided with losers, I thought to myself, "Boy! Are we in deep crap?" Very few of us had any experience running trains over the road, and in six short weeks, they were going to turn us loose across central Minnesota.

After a few weeks of training, most of our guys went to Glencoe to work out of there, running trains down to Minneapolis and St. Paul. A guy named Terry Hanson and I took the job working out of Montevideo, Minnesota. From there, we were supposed to take trains that came from the east, and work the line from Montevideo to Milbank. On the Burlington Northern, this job would have had an engineer, a conductor, and two brakemen. On the TCW, they expected us to get the job done with an engineer and one man to do the work of three. A job that should have taken no more than twelve hours round trip on the BN was taking three and four twelve-hour shifts to complete. The dispatching was terrible, the locomotives were all junk that the BN and other railroads had sold them, and the communications were barely a step ahead of the Pony Express. Most of the time the radios didn't work, so I would have to walk to the nearest telephone, which was often over a couple miles away. Then I'd have to listen to some prima donna dispatcher sitting in an air-conditioned office, bitching about how rough his job was and how the train crews were spoiled and overpaid. We would work twelve hours, then sit there waiting to be relieved for two or three hours, go to a motel for rest, and get called back eight hours later for another twelve-hour shift. All this for a whopping eight dollars and something an hour.

About the time that we were all to be certified as engineers on the TCW, the Burlington Northern called me back. I decided that as bad as it was on the BN, it had to be better than the TCW. In the coming years, the BN would do everything they could to make me regret that decision.

It seemed like the BN was always short of qualified engineers. Every few months they would post a notice that if anyone was interested in becoming an engineer, we could put in a bid. As with everything on the railroad, it was based on seniority. The oldest seniority dates would get the few openings, and they would enter into a six-month training program. After working as a brakeman/switchman and sometimes as a conductor, I thought that it looked pretty good: sitting up in a nice warm locomotive while the other guys were out in the snow and the wind putting the train together. So in 1992, I put in a bid and got accepted into the engineers program.

Along with three guys from Sioux City, Iowa, and one from Minneapolis, I went to work (on-the-job training) riding trains. Depending on the engineer on the job, sometimes I actually got to run the locomotives. This went on for about six weeks and then we were sent down to Overland Park, Kansas, for a couple of weeks of classroom training. They put us through quite a bit, and all in all, it was good training.

I will never forget, one day our instructor asked the class, "What would you do if you were going down a mountain grade with a loaded coal train and you lost your train line air?" One of the guys answered that the first thing he'd do would be to "wake up the conductor, cause he ain't never seen a crash like the one we're gonna have." The instructor failed to see the humor, but it sure cracked up the rest of the class.

At the end of our two weeks we had the opportunity to run trains in the simulator. That was quite an experience, as they were able to throw different scenarios at us and we had to react in a manner that safely prevented any accidents. It also gave us a preview of what we were going to have to pass in order to get our Engineer's license. After our two weeks of training in Overland Park, we headed back home to on-the-job training, this time with more hands-on training. Most of the regular engineers were happy to take trainees because they got a little more pay for each trip. However, some engineers were less than happy about it. Mostly, those were either guys who had been there for forty-some years or those who had recently been promoted and felt like they were irreplaceable.

Toward the end of our six months of training, we went back down to Overland Park and took our written test and our finals on the simulator. We needed a ninety percent for a passing grade. I completed the written test okay, but failed the simulator by just a few points. Fortunately for me, they give us second chances at it and I passed with flying colors that time.

With the way the railroad works, now instead of having a little bit of seniority as a brakeman/switchman, I went to being the engineer with no seniority. This really sucked. If I was lucky enough to hold the extra board, I might work that. Otherwise I would be back as a brakeman/switchman. Frequently, the youngest seniority engineers would get forced to work at Aberdeen, South Dakota, or Minneapolis, neither of which was an assignment that I looked forward to.

Working on the railroad was quite an experience. There were no such things as holidays, birthdays, or graduations, among other things. I often said the only difference between railroading and slavery was that the slaves were eventually freed. Management on the railroad was unbelievable. They expected loyalty and honesty from their employees, but they would say whatever they had to, to get us to work, even if we had not had a day off in weeks.

Trainmasters and other officials would literally lay in the weeds testing us on our train handling skills, and once we were stopped, they would board the train and check out our rule books to make sure that we had all the latest updates and train orders. We referred to them as weed weasels.

The railroad instituted a Four Principles of Safety program in the 1990s which was supposed to impress on us all that there was no such thing as an accident. The fourth principle was that if doing the job involved an unsafe act, that we were required and empowered to cease and desist the activity. This sounded good, but the local railroad management didn't like it when we actually took it literally.

One Sunday afternoon in November, I was called for a job as an engineer to take a van ride along with a conductor and a brakeman out to Beardsley to pull a grain train back out to Morris on the main line—a simple enough task under most conditions. Problem was that it was snowing heavily and we were never allowed to deadhead (travel) by van when it was snowing out. The trainmaster, who shall remain unnamed, insisted that we had to go. So under protest, we piled into the van and headed out. We had not gone a mile out of Willmar when we saw two vehicles in the ditch, and a pickup truck spun out in front of us and nearly hit us head-on. At that point, I told the driver to turn around and go back to the depot. I called the yard master on the radio and told him that we were coming back due to road conditions. He stated that he couldn't give me the authority to do that, and I told him that he didn't have to. The fourth principle of safety covered that.

On our way back in, we met the trainmaster coming out to see how bad it really was. I just waved as he went by. A few minutes later, back in the depot, he came in just fuming. He told us to stick around and he disappeared into his office. Knowing that I had the rule book to back me up, I felt pretty secure. However, a couple of aces up your sleeve never hurts. I called the local sheriff's department and requested the phone numbers of the departments in the two adjoining counties that we would have to go through. Then I called the sheriff's department in Morris and Benson, and asked them about travel conditions. Both of them responded that absolutely no travel was advised. When the trainmaster came back out, he had evidently gotten the same information, as he told us that we could go home. Railroad officials really hate getting their rule book shoved you know where.

As an engineer, our union contract calls for me to get paid for the job that I am called for, even if we are not able to complete it. This would have been a really good payday for me; however, the trainmaster managed to see to it that my time slip never got paid for that trip. Oh well! It was worth it just to show them that someone else knew how to work their rules in their favor, too.

For the most part, working on the railroad was good work. It was just that the management was so anti-employees. It seemed like they would spend thousands of dollars training us to be engineers and from that time on, try to find an excuse to fire us. We often said that the railroad made money in spite of itself, not because of itself.

In spite of the adverse situations that were common, there actually were some good times working on the railroad. During the winter of 1996, we got an unusual amount of snow in Minnesota and the Dakotas. The previous year, the Burlington Northern Railroad and the Santa Fe Railroads had merged, and all of the dispatching had been moved down to Fort Worth, Texas. The dispatchers down there could not understand why we were unable to get our trains through the snow. They had never seen snow drifts twenty feet deep and winds blowing it around at thirty to forty miles per hour. Many trains got stranded and buried in snow drifts and had to be pulled out two or three cars at a time.

As an extra board engineer, I would, on occasion, get called to work a snow plow job. That's where we would take a locomotive and a wedge plow mounted on a railcar and go out to clear the tracks. We usually had a crew of three on the engine and two or three section workers to handle the snow plow. It was rather exciting when we would cut into a drift that was six or eight feet deep and the snow would fly off to the side nearly a hundred feet.

On one morning, we got called to relieve a crew that was coming back into Willmar from out in Watertown, South Dakota. They had been out for a week and were coming back when they ran out of time on their hours of service. (We could work twelve hours and then had to be relieved). We met them in Louisburg, Minnesota, just west of the Minnesota River bottom, near Appleton. Coming down through the bottom was uneventful, but when we started up the hill toward Appleton, we had a deep cut to go through and the snow was drifted in over twenty feet deep.

My conductor and brakeman decided to ride up in the snow plow with section crew so they could see things better. As was the procedure, the section foreman would radio me to come ahead and when to hit reverse and back out before the snow would fall in and trap us. We'd get going about twelve to fourteen miles per hour and go until we'd just about stall out. Then he'd just radio me the command to back out. We would do this continually until we'd finally break through the drift.

On this day, it was not to be. As I sat in the locomotive, I could reach out the window and stick my hand into the wall of snow that towered four to five feet over the top of the locomotive. At one point, we derailed the snow plow, so the section guys had to crawl down and place iron frogs on the rail so that we could re-rail it. With that done, we backed out and hit it again. We had well over a quarter of a mile to go before we could break through to the other side of the drift.

The next time we hit it, we were into the deepest part of the drift. As we hit it, the force of the snow hitting the front of the plow shattered the windshield. The section foreman told me to back out and hit it again. I went up and checked out the damage to the windshield, and after seeing how close it was to caving in all the way, I told him that I would not make another run at it. My reasoning was that if the windshield gave way, there would be an avalanche of snow filling the plow cab and they would all be buried alive in there. With me being the only one in the locomotive, I didn't think it was a very sound move, so we backed out of the drift and called maintenance to see about getting a replacement windshield brought out. Due to the fact that they had to get the replacement windshield out of Minneapolis, they just had us tie the train down and sent a van out to bring us back to Willmar. It's my understanding that they sent a big rotary snow plow out from Willmar to open the drift up from the east end.

Toward the end of March of that year, I was called to work another snow plow job out between Appleton and Watertown. There are quite a few hills out in that area, and every one of the cuts where the tracks ran between the hills had been packed solid with snow. Most were over ten to fifteen feet deep. By this time, the track was open, but we went out with a wedge plow to widen the cuts. We made it out to Watertown and turned around for the return trip the following morning. April 1 turned out to be quite an April Fools' Day. The temperature soared up into the seventies, and the snow melt started running off the hills with a vengeance. When we got east of I-29, we had a small creek to cross. The culvert was washed out and there were three railroad ties that were just hanging by the rail spikes. We stopped to survey the situation and the section foreman insisted that we could get across it. I told him that the only way I would attempt it would be if everyone else got off of the train and went ahead on foot. I figured that if the locomotive went into the creek, there was no sense in having any more people hurt or killed than necessary.

Although I didn't want him there, the section foreman insisted on riding on the step right on the front of the locomotive. If we had gone over, there was no way he'd have made it without being crushed or pinned underwater. We did make it safely across and headed for the Minnesota River valley, quite apprehensive about what we would find there.

The water had come up to the level of the bridge that we had to cross, and it was raging like nothing I had seen for some time. We made it to the other side, but we were the last ones to make it over the bridge that spring. There were two months of serious flooding along the Minnesota River that year, and it took several months after the flood waters receded to rebuild the bridges and the road bed for the tracks running down through the valley.

In 2002, I had been working on the railroad for thirteen years, and the lifestyle of no schedule, being on call twenty-four/seven, not knowing when I was going to work, when I might get to eat, and the lack of proper rest, sitting in a motel room for days on end, was really starting to get to me. Health-wise, it was taking its toll. This was also about the time I was finding myself dealing with things relating to Vietnam. I didn't realize it myself, but other friends of mine who had dealt with it told me that I had Post-Traumatic Stress Disorder (PTSD). Finally, after several months, I went and talked to a representative from the DAV (Disabled American Veterans). They set me up with an appointment at the VA clinic in St. Cloud, Minnesota. Shortly after that, I left my job on the railroad and things have improved ever since.

19

THE LONG ROAD HOME

A FTER THIRTY YEARS OF FIGHTING the demons of my war by myself, I finally realized that it was time to get some help. Like most guys who have been through combat, I knew that I had some problems, but what the hell? I'm a man! I can deal with it. I don't need no shrink trying to get inside my head. The nightmares were coming less frequently, but the other symptoms never seemed to go away. A car would backfire, a gunshot, even the honor guard rifle salute at a funeral would startle me and cause me to look for someplace to take cover.

The VA was a good thing and a bad thing. I started out seeing a female psychologist who decided that I was faking everything, supposedly telling her what I thought that she wanted to hear in order to qualify for PTSD disability. She didn't have a clue about combat and, as far as I was concerned, certainly didn't want to work with combat veterans. In my opinion, the only ones she wanted to help were the female soldiers who had filed claims of sexual harassment. For me, trying to explain to her what combat was like would have been similar to a woman trying to explain to me what the trauma of childbirth was like. She refused to follow the VA guidelines that stated if someone's DD 214 listed a Combat Infantrymen's Badge, a Purple Heart, or a Bronze Star, that was evidence enough that they should be considered for PTSD. Hell, this wasn't something that I wanted; I had been in denial of it for thirty-some years.

After several weeks of being totally stressed out by this person who was assigned to help with my situation, I finally went to the Patient Advocates Office at the VA and requested another psychologist. The lady there was an angel. She set me up with another psychologist who, although he had never been in combat, had made it his mission to learn and to be in a position to help me deal with things. She also put me in touch with a guy from the VA Benefits Office out of St. Paul. John Warren would come out to the VA in St. Cloud once a week and meet with vets who were dealing with claims problems.

The first time that I met John, I was impressed. He was a tall black man with a right arm that was severely injured in combat. Here, finally, I was going to get to talk with a guy who had been there, done that. He'd walked a mile in my shoes, and vise-versa. We talked for over an hour, and he told me that he would do his very best to help me get my claim through the system.

When I got up to leave, he put his good arm around me, gave me a hug, and told me, "Ron, it's good to talk to another real combat soldier." It seemed like he was dealing with a lot of guys who were never in combat, but were claiming all kinds of repercussions from the Vietnam War.

About that same time, I was communicating with a 'Nam veteran from the Willmar area who was working for the St. Paul Veterans Outreach Center. Stan Olson, a Navy Corpsman who served with the Marines in 'Nam, turned out to be a Godsend for me. He would keep tabs on me and the status of my claim with the VA. If things were getting bogged down, he could usually find out where and why.

Just prior to this time, I had started trying to find some of the guys that I remembered from 'Nam. LuWayne "Butch" Schuft was one of the first guys that I tried to find. He and I had both grown up and graduated from Hutchinson High School in Hutchinson, Minnesota. He was two years ahead of me, but his younger brother, Chuck, had graduated with me. Butch and I flew over to 'Nam together, went through Camp Alpha (the replacement center), and were both assigned to the 1st Infantry Division. He went to the 2nd of the 2nd, Mechanized Infantry, and I went to the 1st of the 16th, Mechanized Infantry. Both were headquartered out of Lai Khe. Once we got to Lai Khe, we didn't see each other again until right at the end of our tours. By some stroke of luck, we both ended up in Vung Tau, at an in-country R & R center.

Once we got back to the states, I never saw him again. Then back around 2000, I decided to try to find him. I got ahold of a Hutchinson phone book and started calling all of the Schufts that still lived there. Finally, one lady recommended that I call and talk to the minister of the church where we had both been confirmed. Following her advice, I called the church office. The minister told me that Butch had been called home. For some reason, it didn't register with me right away. Then, like a ton of bricks, it hit me. Butch had died of a massive coronary at the age of fifty-two, just a couple of months before my call.

I decided right then and there, that I was not going to let another one of my friends from 'Nam die without me trying to find them. I knew where Mike Nelson was, and a few of the guys who had gotten together in Anderson, Indiana, back in 1983: guys like David Komes, Dave Jeffrey, Norm Hardin, Jerry Hartman, Gene Zemple, and a few others. At our reunion in Anderson, we all said that we would keep in touch, but with a few exceptions, that didn't happen. Mike Nelson had moved from southeastern Minnesota down to Iowa, started up a tree trimming business, and pretty much dropped out of sight.

In December of 1999, I bought my first computer. Little did I know that it was going to be the tool to help me find and reconnect with many Army friends from the past. The big Y2K scare, the prediction that all of the computers were going to crash and become nonfunctional, never materialized. I figured that if the whole world was going to drop into cyberspace somewhere, then I might as well go with.

Over the next year or two, I got familiar with the internet and learned that I could actually find people that I had been looking for. Michael Tessaro was one of the guys whose family I really felt that I needed to get in touch with. I was with Michael on January 8, 1969, when he died as the result of an attack on our platoon-sized fire base near AnDien, RVN.

All I had to go on was that Michael's home of record was Edwardsville, Indiana. This proved to be incorrect as it really was Edwardsville, Illinois. For years, I had been trying to find relatives of his in Indiana. When I searched the internet, I found a Mike Tessaro in Marysville, Illinois. In November of 2001, I made a phone call to Mike Tessaro. It turned out that this was Michael's father. I could hardly speak; I was so overcome that I was actually talking with Michael's dad. I did manage to tell him that I was with Michael the night he died, and that I would call him back when I could talk. I left him my name and phone number.

Shortly after that, I got a call from Michael's sister, Roseanne. She was wondering who I was and why I was calling. She was just looking out for her father. I managed to tell her all about my connection with Michael and how I had, for many years, been trying to locate them. We called back and forth frequently after that, and my wife and I made plans to drive down and visit them in June of 2002.

Phillip J. Greenwell was another name that kept coming back to me. He was the young twenty-two-year-old company commander for Bandido Charlie Company in July, August, and September, 1969. I had been driving for the previous Company Commander, Captain Kenneth Costich, for three months when Phil took over the Company. I didn't have any information on Cpt. Costich, but I knew that Phil Greenwell was from Johnson City, Tennessee. I searched the white pages and every site on the internet that I could find, and seemed to keep striking out. I found several Phillip Greenwell's, but never the right one.

Then one day in February 2002, I found a Phillip Greenwell in Louisville, Kentucky. I figured, "Oh well, what the heck," I might as well give it a try. I left a message after no one answered, and left my name and number. A couple of days later, I got a call back and it was Phil Greenwell. We were like two kids in a candy store. It was so great to finally reconnect.

Phil was an owner/operator, driving big rigs loaded with hazardous materials all over the United States. After talking with him several times, it was decided that we would swing up to Louisville, Kentucky, after our stop at Tessaros. Phil mentioned that he had also just recently heard from a Doug Ludlow from Michigan. Doug was with our fourth (weapons) platoon and was with us on August 12, 1969, when I was wounded for the second time. I called Doug and we started pooling our information. As time went on, we found a few more guys. They each knew one or two others and we just kept adding to our list of Bandidos.

At some point during this time, I came into contact with Curtis Hatterman. He had been with Bandido Charlie Company when they were with the 9th Division and came up to the 1st Division in the big swap. Curtis was a wealth of information. He had a Bandido Charlie website, and he was probably the one key link that helped bring the Bandidos back together again. Curtis lived in Enid, Oklahoma, but he had roots back up in my area. His grandfather was from the Kandiyohi/Atwater area and he had gone to St. John's Lutheran Church just north of Atwater.

Curt and I became good friends, and even though we didn't really remember each other from 'Nam, we served in the same unit at the same time. Just prior to my arrival into the country, Curtis was wounded and two others killed when someone mistook them for enemy soldiers. They were on an LP (listening post) just outside of the wire, huddled in a bomb crater, when one of our own guys fired an M-79 grenade round at them. On September 20, 1968, PFC William R. Moreledge was killed, and SPC 4 Douglas K. Baron died shortly after midnight. His date of death is listed as September 21, 1968. Their names can be found on The Wall. Panel number 43 W, lines 48 and 51. Curtis dealt with a lot of survivor's guilt from this incident. His last four months in 'Nam were spent back at Lai Khe.

In June 2002, Janet and I made a road trip to see a bunch of my old Army buddies. Our first stop was Coralville, Iowa, where we visited with Mike and Kathy Nelson. It had been thirty years since Mike and I had gotten together. Back in 1972, I had called him to ask about he and Goldie getting together with Janet and me somewhere for a little mini-reunion. His next comment just about knocked me to the floor. He said, "Oh, you haven't heard? Goldie was killed in a car accident in May of 1971." To say that I was devastated would be an understatement. After surviving a year of combat in Vietnam, to come home and get killed by a drunk driver seemed like such a waste of life. Goldie had gotten married, and as things turned out, his wife, who survived the crash, was pregnant. From what I had heard, Goldie never knew this, as she was in the early stages of the pregnancy.

Mike Nelson (Caledonia, MN), Ron Mackedanz, and Greg "Goldie" Goldenstein (Fifty Lakes, MN). Minnesota buddies in AnDien, South Vietnam, January 1969.
(Photo from the author's collection.)

In 1972, Janet and I had gone down to Caledonia to visit with Mike Nelson and his wife, Kathy, for a couple of days, but it seemed like we had very little in common. I don't know if it was because of Goldie's death, or just the directions that each of our lives had taken, but it just didn't seem like what either of us thought it would be like. We stayed in touch somewhat over the years, but it wasn't until I called and told him about our proposed road trip in 2002 that we finally got together. Mike was originally from Caledonia, Minnesota, and we both got to 'Nam around the middle of October, 1968. We served in the second platoon together until I got assigned to drive the Company Commander's track. I think that Mike's wife, Kathy, was a little apprehensive about old war wounds being drug up again, but things went really well. We had a really great visit with them, got to meet their kids, Patrick and Dee, and their spouses.

Then on Sunday, June 16, which happened to be Father's Day, we arrived down at Tessaros. WOW! If I have never done anything good in my life, this was to be it. Mike and his family welcomed us into their home and treated us like family. I felt like I was the prodigal son, returned home. We spent two days down there with them. Mike, Janet, and I went out to the cemetery and visited Michael's gravesite. We placed some flags, I spent some time alone at the gravesite, and we took a few pictures. With the exception of a letter from one of our officers in 'Nam, I was the only one who ever contacted the family in the thirty years since Michael's death.

The next day, one of Mike's granddaughters asked us if we would be willing to talk with a reporter from the Collinsville newspaper. They were very interested in the fact that after nearly thirty-four years, someone who had been with Michael in 'Nam had come forth. Mike and I went in and met with a staff writer by the name of Rebecca B. Gedda. She did a really nice article about our meeting, and it was on the front page of the June 19 issue of the Collinsville Herald Journal. When she was wrapping up her interview with us, she asked Mike, "What was the most meaningful thing that you have gotten out of this meeting with

Ron?" He answered her, as he choked back the tears. "Just knowing that someone was with Michael when he died."

Michael was married when he died. After his funeral, the Tessaro family had very little contact with his widow. The information that I received was that she had remarried and moved away. All Michael's dad had were two South Vietnamese medals, and he didn't know what they were. As it turned out, one was the Cross of Gallantry and the other was the Civil Actions Medal. I was able to help Mike get in touch with the right people and he received a duplicate set of Michael's medals.

Over the past few years, I stayed in touch with Michael's family. His father passed away in 2007, but I still keep in contact with Michael's sister, Roseanne, on occasion.

When we left Tessaro's, we headed down to Cleveland, Tennessee. My wife had an aunt down there who she had never met, and I had plans to hook up with another Bandido. Rufus Hood had been with the Bandidos about the same time that I was there. He was wounded sometime around the first of the year in 1969 and managed to get on as the company clerk. I don't recall him from our time over there, but then I never spent much time in the rear, at least not until I was released from the hospital in September, 1969.

Rufus was working for the FBI when we met in June 2002. We shared some pictures and some stories, but at the time it didn't seem like we had that much in common, other than the fact that we each served with the same unit in 'Nam. Several of us have urged Rufus to attend some of the reunions, but so far it's been a no-go. Hopefully, he will show up one of these days.

From there, we headed up to Louisville, Kentucky. Other than my time in Fort Campbell, Kentucky, I had never seen much of that part of the country. The drive from Cleveland, Tennessee, to Louisville was beautiful. When we got to Louisville, Phil Greenwell and his wife had just moved into a new home. They were in the midst of just getting settled in.

The last time that I had seen Phil was in Lai Khe, RVN, back in September of 1969. Man, was it great to see him again!

We had so much to talk about and we didn't waste any time getting to it. I remember that the Bandidos had finally come in for a few days to relax and resupply after Operation Kentucky Cougar. From Phil's place, we headed up to my brother Neal's, up in Findlay, Ohio.

On the way, we stopped in briefly and visited with Dave Jeffrey and his wife, Roseanne. We had dinner with them and then headed north. Time was running short, and we had a couple stops to make and many miles to drive. Neal and his family lived in an old church that they were remodeling into a home. It sort of reminded me of the Arlo Guthrie song about Alice's Restaurant, where Alice lived in a church.

While planning our trip, I had talked with another Bandido from Ohio. Herb McHenry lived in Wadsworth, near Akron. Herb met us in Willard, Ohio. As is so often the case, I didn't remember Herb from 'Nam, but he had served in the second platoon after I went to the Command track. We had many shared experiences, including the big firefight on August 12.

As we sat in the Legion Club at Willard and talked, my brother, Neal, sat quietly just soaking it all in. This was the first time that he had ever heard me talk about 'Nam. When we parted company that day, Herb and I had rekindled a camaraderie that can only be shared by men who have fought in combat together. This was to be the first of several meetings.

Janet and I spent the evening and part of the next day with Neal and his family before we ventured north to Michigan. Doug Ludlow's was our next stop, at Battle Creek. Doug owns and operates a very successful landscaping business in Battle Creek. We spent the night with Doug and his wife, Catherine, and then we headed north to their cabin in central Michigan.

This was to be the point of a mini reunion of sorts. Several old Bandidos live in Michigan: Al Kalchik, Norm Hardin, Ben McGeachy, Jerry Gore, and a few others. At the time, we had located Al and Norm, who were coming up to the cabin. Also, one of the guys who served with Doug in the fourth platoon was driving up from Arkansas with a medic from Alpha Company who was with us on August 12. Roger Haynie and Mike "Doc" Askew made the venture north. We had a great time at the cabin and it was great seeing those guys after all those years. Doc had a small eighteen-by-twenty-four inch American flag that had flown on one of the Alpha Company tracks on August 12. It had several bullet holes and a few blood stains on it. He had framed it up and brought it along to show us.

After over a week on the road, Janet and I were looking forward to getting back home. We decided to head west, over to Ludington, Michigan, to catch the ferry boat that crosses Lake Michigan over to Manitowoc, Wisconsin. As it turned out, Al Kalchik's father-in-law was the Captain on the SS Badger for many years. He had recently retired so we didn't get the chance to meet him, but one of Al's daughters worked in the gift shop on the ferry. The trip took four hours to complete, but it saved us the hassle of having to deal with the traffic around Chicago.

As we traveled through Wisconsin on our last leg of the trip, we stopped at "The High Ground" near Neillsville. This is a memorial to veterans of all wars, with an emphasis placed on the Native American culture. If ever in that part of Wisconsin, make sure to stop and see it. It is very unique and well worth the stop.

20

THE WALL

A FTER OUR ROAD TRIP IN JUNE 2002, we went to New Orleans for the First Infantry Division Reunion. There were only a handfull of Bandidos there: Phil Greenwell, Doug Ludlow, Roger Haynie, Mike "Doc" Askew, and me. It was a great time, spending a few days with these guys again.

One afternoon as we were sitting around in the 16th Infantry CP (command post), I noticed a WWII vet sitting all by himself, watching us talk, laugh, and have fun. He was smiling and seemed to be enjoying us renewing old friendships. After a while, I went over and introduced myself and we struck up a conversation. His name was Art Betancourt. He was a WWII vet and most of his buddies that used to come to the reunions were either too ill to travel or had passed on. Art still had a twinkle in his eye and I could tell that he enjoyed just being there. He asked me if I wanted to see a picture of his girlfriend. Then he pulled out an old black and white photo of a young gal, probably around twenty years old, in a one piece bathing suit. She was very good looking. It was his wife of many years, Adeline.

During the banquet, one of the other guys in the 16th Infantry Regiment, Dennis Moorehead, came over and said that he had someone from Charlie Company 1st of the 16th (Mech) at their table. I went with him and sure enough, there was Phil (Norman) Ardoin and his wife, Kristie, from Ville Platte, Louisiana. Naturally, I invited them to join us at our table. After the banquet, they had a dance with music provided by Phil Greenwell. Most of the people didn't stick around for the dance, but seeing as how Phil was doing the music, we decided to stay and enjoy ourselves. One lady that was out on the floor was Adeline Betancourt. It turns out that she had been a dance instructor and really loved to dance. I even had the pleasure of a dance with her. Her husband, Art, had suffered a stroke the previous summer and was not able to get around very well. However, when they played a slow dance, Adeline got him out on the dance floor. I took a picture of them dancing cheek to cheek and sent them a framed copy of it. The Betancourts were a neat couple, always fun to be around.

Phil Greenwell introduced us to General James Hollingsworth and his lovely wife, Janie. General Hollingsworth was the Assistant Division Commander of the 1st Infantry Division during part of our time in Vietnam. Of course at the time, I didn't know who the Division officers were, and really didn't have a need to know. General Hollingsworth was very humble, but still carried that command presence about him. He told us all how much respect he had for us and how he was proud to have served with us. His wife was the typical sweet little southern belle. She accompanied the General wherever he went and wore white evening gloves. Why I remember that, I'll never know.

After returning from New Orleans, I was riding an emotional high. It was so great getting together again. About three weeks later, my mood went right in the tank. It's hard to explain, but after taking part in all that went on in New Orleans, I suppose that I should have expected something like that. I started going to the VA more regularly, and they finally diagnosed me with PTSD.

During these visits to the VA, I had several C and Ps (compensation and pension exams). One of the doctors that I had to see was a Dr. Nyugen. I hate to admit it, but I copped an attitude right away. I thought to myself, "Great, just what I need, a Vietnamese doctor." It turned out that he was an officer in the South Vietnamese Army and he ran a field hospital near Lai Khe, the same area that I was in during my year in 'Nam. Once we found a little common ground, I found out that he was a pretty good doctor. Thanks to him, my disability for my wounds was upgraded to thirty percent from the ten percent that I had been receiving since I was discharged. After all these years, I still have small pieces of shrapnel surfacing in my back, and another fair-sized piece lodged in my left thigh. In September 2003, the VA rated me at one hundred percent disabled due to a combination of things relating to my Vietnam service. Since that time, I have been disability retired and finally enjoying life.

After attending the Big Red One reunion in New Orleans, I was anxious for the next one. It was held in Reno, Nevada, and we had twenty-two Bandidos attend. For many of the guys, it was the first time they had seen one another since 'Nam. Lieutenant Colonel Kenneth Cassels (our former battalion commander) came. He later said that he was somewhat hesitant about coming, not knowing if the men would want to see him or not. His fears were unjustified. He was welcomed with open arms and treated like a Bandido. His wife, Peggy, had a birthday during the reunion. Ken got a cake and we all held a big surprise birthday party for her.

It was at this reunion that word had gotten out that I was writing a newsletter for the Bandidos of Charlie Company 1st of the 16th (Mech) Infantry. Dennis Moorehead, one of the association officers, asked me if I would help with the association newsletter, the *Dagwood Dispatches*. I told him that my basket was full at the time with other things that I was involved with, but that I would talk with him the following year about it. The Honorary Colonel of the Regiment, Jerry Griffin, was doing the newsletter and he needed some help with it.

In October 2003, we received word that Gilbert "Doc" Thompson's niece had been killed while serving with the Wisconsin National Guard in Iraq. I had met Gil and his wife, Janeen, in Reno just a month earlier at the BRO reunion. When we heard about Rachel's death, I told my wife that we needed to go over to Berlin, Wisconsin, for the funeral. When I told Gil that we were coming, he was very pleased. As it turned out, there were four of us from Bandido Charlie there: Doug Ludlow, Mike Renshaw, Phil Greenwell, and me. We were not there to make a spectacle, but all of Gil's relatives mentioned how great it was that his buddies from Vietnam had come to be with him at this time of sorrow and grief. The morning of the funeral as I was sitting in the motel lobby, the words to a verse came into my head. I took a pen and paper and wrote "Daddy's Little Soldier Girl" that morning. The day we buried Rachel Bosveld would have been her twentieth birthday.

December 2003 found me making another trip east. This time, back to Doug Ludlow's place in Battle Creek, Michigan. Doug had a 2000 Harley Road King that he wanted to sell. His new 2004 model had just come in and he was looking for a home for the old one. For many years I had dreamed of owning a Harley, and when Doug told me that his was for sale, I jumped at it. I had a little money saved up and decided to buy it. We stayed at Doug and Catherine's overnight, and the next day I took the Harley out for a little road test. When I came back, I ran it up in the trailer, handed Doug a cashier's check for the Harley, and we headed back to Minnesota.

All winter long, Doug kept e-mailing me about riding to Washington, D.C. in May for the big Vietnam veteran's motorcycle ride to The Wall called "Rolling Thunder." Although I had owned a few motorcycles before, I never had anything that I could take a long trip on. As soon as the weather warmed up in March, I got the Harley out and started riding. I wanted to get a few miles under my belt before embarking on a big trip like that.

When I left home on the Harley it was forty-five degrees and threatening rain. I headed down through the Twin Cities and into Wisconsin. My first stop was at the High Ground Memorial in Neillsville.

Then it was on to Gil and Janeen Thompson's place where I would spend the night. The following morning, Gil took me over for a tour of Nueske's, which is a meat processing business that

The author, Ron Mackedanz, at the High Ground Memorial in
Neillsville, WI, in May 2004 on the way out to Rolling Thunder.
(Photo from the author's collection.)

makes the best apple-smoked bacon and hams that you can find
anywhere. Gil works for them and travels all over the U.S. pro-
moting their products.

I left Gil's place around noon for the short ride down to
Manitowoc, Wisconsin, where I would take the ferry boat across
the lake over to Al Kalchik's place in Ludington, Michigan. Al was
the fifty gunner on the command track on August 12, 1969, when
we got into that firefight with the North Vietnamese Army. I spent
the night with the Kalchik's and had a great visit.

The next morning, I headed for Lansing, Michigan, to meet
up with another old 2nd platoon Bandido. The temperature
down along Lake Michigan was thirty-five degrees, a bit chilly for
motorcycle riding, but it warmed up quickly as I got away from
the lake. Ben McGeachy was one of the guys who had been
through "Tet of 1968" with the Bandidos while they were still
part of the 9th Division. He was a few years older than most of

us in 'Nam, probably around twenty-four years old, which made him an old guy. Ben drove the track for the 2nd squad, of the 2nd platoon, and this is where I was assigned. Ben taught me all about driving tracks and how to maintain them so that they were ready to roll out when needed. I met Ben at a Cracker Barrel restaurant in Lansing for coffee and rolls and we had a short visit, as he was just on break from work. As with the others, it was great to see him again.

Later that afternoon, I rode into Battle Creek, Michigan, and met up with Doug Ludlow. We spent the night at his place, and sometime around 6:00 a.m. we rolled out to see how many deer we could dodge on our way over to meet a couple of his friends who would be riding with us. We rode from Battle Creek to Clarksburg, West Virginia, that day. As I recall, it took us around fourteen hours of riding time. I was really getting broken in on this road tripping by motorcycle.

Once we got to Clarksburg, we hooked up with several other Bandidos who would be making the ride to The Wall with us: Mike and Sue Renshaw, Don Lane and LuAnn O'Dell, Phil Greenwell, Steve Biernacki, Roger Haynie, and a few other friends. The trip in from Clarksburg was beautiful, riding through the mountains of West Virginia. It still took the better part of the day to get to Fairfax, Virginia, where we had hotel reservations.

Janet and Doug's wife, Catherine, both came in by plane that evening. We all got together on a patio at the hotel and had pizza and beer. After that, it was time to turn in early. We needed to hit the road by 5:00 a.m. the next morning to get over to the North Pentagon parking lot before the big crowds started arriving. As we rode in, there were already over ten thousand motorcycles there. We pulled up in line with the others and mingled around, watched others come in, and some of us even managed a nap. It was quite a sight, watching as the endless line of motorcycles kept coming and coming. The ride was scheduled to start at noon, and by that time, they had registered over 400,000 motorcycles. Yes, that's right, over four hundred thousand. Lucky for us that we had gotten there early.

At noon, they released a big bunch of balloons to signify the start of the ride. Surprisingly, things went very smoothly and we were on the street by 12:30 or so. We pulled out and rode four abreast down the streets of Washington, D.C. As we crossed the Potomac River Bridge, we saw Gil and Janeen Thompson. There were people lined up on both sides waving and wishing us well. A lot of "welcome homes" were heard. For some of us, this really was the welcome home parade that we never had. Wow! It was breathtaking. People lined up six deep on each side of the road for most of the route to The Wall, many trying to reach out and slap our hands, wishing us well, and thanking us for our service. It got to a point where I had to have my wife handle that job, as we were riding very slowly and it took all I could do to keep the Harley upright.

At several intersections along the route, there would be a lone Marine, in full dress uniform standing at attention, saluting the riders. If there was a Marine on the ride with a dry eye, I'd be very surprised. Hell, I had tears in my eyes most of the way. Once we got to the parking area, things got confusing. As it turned out, Mike Renshaw had dropped out of the ride with throttle cable problems. No one seemed to know where he was. Finally we located him and some of the guys helped him get going again.

Next came The Wall, the much anticipated, but somewhat dreaded, destination for our trip. After thirty-five years, to finally be there was very emotional. I had looked up the names of Michael Tessaro, my cousin Lyle Mackedanz, and several others. The weekend that we were there was the same weekend that the WWII Memorial had been dedicated, just the previous day. The crowd that day was enormous, but when we got over by The Wall, everyone was quiet. It was as though we were on hallowed ground.

Janet was with me, but she hung back, allowing me my space and time alone with my friends on The Wall. As I was sitting there on my knees with Michael Tessaro's name right in front of me, a WWII vet came by. He put his hand softly on my shoulder and said something that I'll never forget, "You guys had it a lot rougher that we did during WWII." I am not sure that was the case for all, but for some it may have been. Just to hear those words from a WWII vet held a lot of meaning.

I stopped and visited at Lyle's name for a while, finally completing a mission that I had wanted to do for many years. As a light mist started to fall, Janet and I headed back for the Harley and returned to the hotel.

That evening, we all went out for dinner accompanied by Wendy Winslow. He was the Company Commander of Bandido Charlie when the move was made from the 9th Division to the 1st Division in September 1968. Wendy and his wife, Jeanie, live and work in the D.C. area and came over to meet up with us that evening. What a day! Washington, D.C. for the first time in my life, the Rolling Thunder ride, The Wall, and the whole experience with brothers in arms from 'Nam. This was indeed an experience of a lifetime.

The next morning being Memorial Day, some of us had planned to go over to the Big Red One memorial to attend the ceremonies over there, but after sending our wives to the airport, taking group pictures, and saying goodbye to those heading in other directions, we just didn't get over there in time.

Mike Renshaw, Doug Ludlow, Steve Biernacke, and I on our Harleys, and Roger Haynie in his pickup truck, headed north through Baltimore on our way up to Lebanon, Pennsylvania, to see another Bandido, Phil Arnold. On our ride through Baltimore, it rained cats and dogs. Being a fairly new rider, this really had me puckered up. Raining to beat heck and cars flying by going seventy-five miles an hour was not my idea of a good time. Once we got north of Baltimore, the rain let up and we all made it safely to Phil and Sandy's that evening in time for a fantastic meal cooked by Phil. We all had a great time that evening, telling lies and swearing to it. Roger and Steve, who served on the same

Bandidos in Washington, D.C. for Rolling Thunder, May 2004. Left to Right: Gilbert (Doc) Thompson, Mike & Susan Renshaw, Don Lane & LuAnn Odell, Phil Greenwell, Janeen Thompson, Marv Bosveld, Ed Chaffin, Roger Haynie, Doug & Catherine Ludlow, Keith & Shelly Killam, Steve Beirnacke and Ron Mackedanz
(Notes: Marv Bosveld is Gil Thompsons nephew and the father of Rachel Bosveld who was KIA in Iraq on 26 Oct. 2003. Keith and Shelly Killan are Marv's niece and nephew.)
(Photo from the author's collection.)

track with Doug Ludlow, were going at it with a verbal battle like they were going to kill each other. Fortunately, it was all in good fun. The following day, we all split up to go our separate directions. Steve Biernacke and I rode up to Wilkes-Barre, Pennsylvania, where he lived and from there, I continued on. My new destination was the VA hospital in White River Junction, Vermont.

Having never been in New England, this was quite an experience. To be going it alone on a Harley was a dream come true. My reason for going there was Chuck Richards. We had served together in 'Nam and when he returned stateside, he came to Fort Carson, Colorado, and we were in the same outfit. We had maintained contact throughout the years, and Chuck and a buddy of his had ridden out to our place in Minnesota back in 1987 and stayed with us for a few days. Now Chuck was in the VA hospital in White River Junction, virtually on his death bed.

I had been planning to make the trip up to his place in New Hampshire when I came out for Rolling Thunder, but my plans got changed with this development. I pulled in to the VA hospital around seven o'clock that evening. The hospital staff let me see Chuck. At the time, he was pretty much out of it. I really don't even think that he knew I was there. He was very jaundiced and they said that his liver function was down to five percent. The odds were not in his favor.

I left the hospital knowing full well that I had seen my friend alive for the last time. Before leaving the area, I rode over to Lebanon, New Hampshire, mainly just so that I could say I'd been to New Hampshire. The trip back through Vermont and eastern New York State was breathtaking. What beautiful country. I stopped at a Harley shop in Fort Ann, New York, to get the oil changed in the Harley, and bought a t-shirt. Doesn't everybody? Then I headed south and west through upstate New York.

The next stop on my journey was Camillus, New York, and Mike Renshaw's place. I spent the night there, and the following morning Mike rode with me for an hour or so before dropping off. I traveled through western New York, northwestern Pennsylvania, and into Ohio. I rode to Wadsworth, Ohio, where I spent the night with Bandido Herb McHenry and his wife, Joanne. The next day it was off to Findlay, Ohio, to meet my brother Neal for breakfast. Wanting to get to Mike Nelson's place in Iowa that night, I didn't spend much time with Neal. I had many miles to go to get to Coralville, Iowa. As things turned out, it was getting dark and my low beam was burned out, so I got a motel room in Moline, Illinois, and continued my journey to Nelson's the following day. As I recall, I spent a couple nights there and then hit the road for my final leg of the trip. When I arrived home, I had put 3,800 miles on my Harley in thirteen days. What an experience.

In the fall of 2004, Doug Ludlow and Curtis Hatterman were recognized as Distinguished Members of the Regiment by the 16th Infantry Regiment Association. The investiture took place at Fort Riley, Kansas. I decided to go down and see these two friends of mine as they were inducted. This was my first time on a military base since back in 1970 when I left Fort Carson, never once looking back. Fort Riley had come a long way from what I had heard it was back in the sixties and seventies. It had been built up quite a bit and was actually pretty nice. We had the opportunity to hang with the active duty Iron Rangers of the 1st Battalion, 16th Infantry (mech). We watched them go through some training maneuvers, saw some of the weapons being used these days, and sat in on some briefings. The second day there, we all sat in as Doug, Curtiss, and three others were inducted as Distinguished Members of the Regiment.

Curtis Hatterman receiving his Distinguished Member of the Regiment honors. October 2004.
(Photo from the author's collection.)

Doug Ludlow receiving his Distinguished Member of the Regiment
honors. October 2004.
(Photo from the author's collection.)

The final evening there, we attended a formal Military
Ball, the first one that I had ever been to. This was quite interesting. They recognized the new DMORs, presented several awards
to soldiers for exemplary performance, and presented a check to
the 1st Battalion, Iron Rangers, from the 16th Infantry Regiment
Association. They did a Grog ceremony, where they have a huge
punch bowl, and in turn, soldiers go up and pour the contents
from a bottle of whatever represented each war that the Regiment had fought in. After pouring most of the contents into the
punch bowl, the soldier doing the honors would then down the
remaining liquid from the bottle, usually to the applause of his
fellow soldiers of his unit. In some cases, an old sweaty sock or
other GI garment might be dipped in the grog, then stirred with
the butt of a rifle. At that point, a high ranking NCO or an Officer
would taste test the grog to see if it was fit for human consump-
tion. In most cases it was deemed to be missing something, and
after the necessary component was added, it was ready for dis-
tribution to the tables.

The junior soldier at each table was obliged to run up and fill his pitcher with the grog before it was all gone. Upon his return to his table, he would charge the glasses of those seated at his table and everyone present would stand and a toast would be made. "First to the United States, second, to the Commander in Chief, third, to the Army, fourth, to the Big Red One, fifth, to the Regiment, sixth, to the DMORs, seventh, to the ladies, and finally, a toast to our fallen comrades."

Once the banquet meal was served and the guest speaker had presented his speech, the Ball would begin. It was fun watching the young soldiers and their ladies in their fancy gowns out on the dance floor.

Shortly after the DMOR ceremony in 2004, Phil Greenwell told us that he was going to Iraq. He felt like he had to do something and the military wouldn't have him at his age, so he went to work for a contractor, driving fuel trucks out of Baghdad. A nice, safe little task—NOT! Fortunately, Phil completed his year in Iraq, and with the urging of his eighty-something-year-old mother Eloise, and his newfound love, Linda, they were able to convince him not to extend his contract. Phil was able to take a leave from Iraq and come home for the 1st Division reunion in 2005. This gave me and Janet a chance to meet Linda, and she accompanied us around the sights of D.C.

The BRO reunion in 2005 was held in Arlington, Virginia, right next to Washington, D.C. This gave me another chance to visit The Wall. I went through a list that we had of all the guys from Bandido Charlie Company, both 9th Division and 1st Division, who were killed in 'Nam. Between January 1967 and March 1970, we lost fifty-seven men from our unit: dead. I decided to make up some little placards to place along The Wall near each one's name, showing their name, home of record, date of death, and placement on The Wall. Each of the three days that we were there, I got up at around 5:00 a.m. and went over to The Wall, and as I placed the placard with their name on it, I ran my fingers across their engraved name to let them know that they will never be forgotten.

On the last day that we were there, Gil Thompson asked me if he and his daughter, Sarah, could go with me. I told him that if they could be up by five o'clock the next morning, they most certainly were welcome to come along. Sarah is a very accomplished photographer and she shot many photos of Gil and I placing the placards that morning. One of the most breathtaking shots that she captured was the reflection of Gil and I on The Wall with the Red, White and Blue waving proudly on a flag pole that is right between us.

Reflection of Ron Mackedanz and Gil (Doc) Thompson at The Wall during the Big Red One reunion, 2005.
(Photo courtesy of Studio One Eleven photographer Sarah Orlando.)

In October 2005, one of my former Company Commanders, Sherwood "Woody" Goldberg, my 1st Sergeant, Al Herrera, and I were all inducted as Distinguished Members of the Regiment. This is quite an honor, as there are only about 135 living DMORs. To be held in such high esteem by your fellow brothers in arms is very special. Janet and our youngest daughter, Dawna, accompanied me for this presentation. Dawna caused quite a stir the night of the Ball when she came walking in with a long, beautiful red gown on. She turned the head of every soldier in the banquet hall.

Sarah Orlando (Gil and Janeen Thompson's daughter) and Ron
Mackedanz at The Wall in July 2005.
(Photo courtesy of Studio One photographer Sarah Orlando.)

21

STRAIGHT FROM THE GUT

THE FOLLOWING VERSES were written by a combat-wounded veteran of the Vietnam War. I spent ten months of my year-long tour of duty out in the field serving with "Bandido Charlie Company" 1st of the 16th (mechanized) Infantry. I was wounded twice in combat against the Viet Cong and the NVA.

If anyone is offended by any of these writings, deal with it. We all did, in 'Nam. I make no apologies, and I ask no quarter.

Forty-some years later, a lot of this is just now coming to a head. Most Vietnam vets have gone on with their lives, married, taken on respectable work and tried to put it all behind them. Those who believe that they have accomplished that mission are either fooling themselves, or trying to find peace in the bottom of a bottle.

War is hell and combat is a M----- F-----. That's just a fact of life. Combat will change a person forever, and not necessarily for the better. However, life must go on.

These memories and verses are dedicated to Ron's cousin, SFC Lyle Mackedanz, MIA/POW, Vietnam, April 21, 1968, and to all the Bandidos and other brave men who gave their all in a far away land called Vietnam.

This verse was written after I visited the family of Michael J.Tessaro in June 2002. Michael was a friend of mine. On January 8, 1969, our platoon-sized base camp came under attack by the Viet Cong. Michael, myself, and several others were wounded that night. Michael died at my feet on the medevac flight to Lai Khe. It took thirty-three years for me to finally meet with Michael's father and other family members.

Finest Son

The year was 1968, and into Sixty-nine.
Brave young soldiers wrote letters home.
Said, "Mom, I'm doing fine."

When in reality, things were not so well.
From the rice paddies and the jungles,
war was a living hell.

On January 8th of Sixty-nine, Michael Tessaro died.
Some men held their heads, and some men even cried.

One of America's finest sons,
and a brother to us all,
now lies at rest in his families plot.
His name is on The Wall.
His name is on The Wall.

(07/2002)

This verse was written in July of 2002 after visiting the gravesite of Michael J. Tessaro, with his father, Mike Tessaro. Michael is buried in his family plot, near his mother and other family members.

Far and Distant Shores

In nineteen hundred and sixty-eight,
brave young men flew off to war.
To fight and die for freedom,
on some far and distant shore.

As their fathers had before them gone, in 1942,
they shed their blood, and some men died.
Just for me and you.

Now under God, this great nation stands.
A tribute to them all.
When our country needs brave men to fight,
our best will answer the call.

Some will return to enjoy a life,
with their family and a wife.
Grateful, now we all should be,
to those who gave their life.

(07/2002)

In the winter of 2002-2003, as I was dealing with the effects of PTSD (Post-Traumatic Stress Disorder), the next verse was written. Although most of us try our best to hide it and deal with it "like a man," it sometimes is not all that easy. From time to time, it seems that the Vietnam War manages to raise its ugly head and we are forced to deal with it, all over again.

The War Iniside
In nineteen hundred and sixty-eight,
I went off to Vietnam.
My mother said, "Be careful son."
All I could say was, "Yes Mom."

Then I hurried off to that distant land,
to draw my combat pay.
The things I saw each night and day,
would make an atheist pray.

I made some friends, I watched some die.
The war made my blood run cold.
We tried to say, "It don't mean nothing."
But that story's getting old.

Those of us who made it home,
still fight the war, inside.
Everyday, our thoughts return,
to friends of ours, who died.

(12/28/2002)

Nobody

Nobody seems to understand the things we've seen and done.
The price we paid for freedom, in a war that couldn't be won.

In every waking hour, of every fateful day,
if they knew what thoughts go through our heads,
they would lock us up and throw the key away.

For those of us who fought that war, the end is not in sight.
It seems each day we must relive the carnage of the fight.

For thirty years we've gotten by, thanks to the ones we love.
For thirty more we hope to go, with the help of the Lord above.

(01-05-2003)

Drafted

The next two verses were written to honor the memories of the many Vietnam vets who came home from an unpopular war and went on with their lives. As most 'Nam vets, they just faded away into society. Many of them have passed on since returning from Vietnam. Most we have not seen since our time in the rice paddies and the jungles of Vietnam. Each and every one of them deserves our respect and admiration.

Quietly

Quietly, they've come and gone,
names and faces from the past.
No marching bands, no bugler's call,
they have found their peace at last.

In a distant land, we fought a war,
unpopular to some.
We proudly answered freedom's call,
in our hearts, we know we won.

Now as we answer our maker's call,
to enter heaven's gate.
Triumphantly, onward they go,
while quietly, we wait.

(01/07/2003)

Their Names Aren't On The Wall

These men, we knew in Vietnam.
Bandidos, one and all.
Gallantly, we fought the enemy.
As Bandidos, we stood tall.

When their year was up,
we said good-bye, to those returning home.
And now we try to remember them,
in the words of this simple poem.

The Lord has called these brave men home.
They are heroes, one and all.
In our memories, they will always live,
though their names aren't on The Wall.

(01/07/2003)

During the spring and summer of 2003, many Vietnam combat veterans continued to try to work through their PTSD problems and just keep going. I wrote this next verse while waiting to talk to John Warren at the St. Cloud VA Medical Center. John was a benefits representative with the VA, a combat-wounded veteran, a Marine, and a man who understood. He has indeed walked a mile in our boots. Thanks, John.

Scars

The scars I bare are not self-inflicted.
The letter that came in '68 said, "You have been selected."
Called to fight a war in a foreign land, for reasons that I didn't understand.

"War is Hell," combat soldiers say. Some die, others live to fight another day.
In Vietnam, if you survived, one day, on the Freedom Bird you would fly.

Now, the combat is over, but the battles rage. It seems they just get worse with age.
Family and friends don't understand, how my life was changed in Vietnam.

They say that we must put it all behind,
but it's hard to erase what's locked in your mind.
I pray each night that I will pass this test, and to the Lord, I'll give the rest.

The load we carry is heavy still, the choice was simple, kill or be killed.
I'll find my way through and this too shall pass.
Thanks to the people who stood by me,
and the rest of the world can kiss my ass.
(05/14/2003)

After attending the eighty-fifth annual reunion of the 1st Infantry Division (The Big Red One) in Reno, Nevada, in July, 2003, I realized that I was not alone in my battle with PTSD. Many other combat vets are dealing with the same set of problems. Working through the VA and talking with other 'Nam vets, it became very evident that many vets are in a state of denial. Like any other problem, first we have to address the fact that we have a problem.

Reach out, my brother, for you are not alone.

You Are Not Alone

Throughout life's many struggles, we wander aimlessly.
Though friends and love forsake us, internally, we bleed.

They say, we never wanted to talk about it. Hell! They never
gave us a chance.
The world just went and passed us by, without a backward
glance.

Most of us sought nothing. Our government let us down.
They left us all to struggle, like some wounded circus clown.

Now the time has come to pay the fiddler, and they are dancing
to our tune.
Johnny is finally comin' home.
And you are not alone.

(10/29/2003)

This verse was written on November 7, 2003. This day would have been the twentieth birthday of PFC Rachel Bosveld. Instead, it was the day that she was buried with full military honors in Berlin, Wisconsin.

Rachel was the grandniece of one of my Vietnam vet buddies, Gilbert (Doc) Thompson. When news reached us of Rachel's tragic death in Iraq, I knew immediately that I would have to be there for the services. Rachel proudly served with the Army's 527th Military Police in Baghdad, Iraq.

I penned this verse on the morning of her funeral, and read it privately to her family later in the day.

May the Lord keep Rachel safe in his arms. God bless.

Daddy's Little Soldier Girl

Who would have ever thought it, as we watched her grow and play?
That daddy's little girl would go off to war one day?

She grew up with good values, God, family and freedom for all.
The day she put on that uniform, so proudly she stood tall.

In the early spring of the year '03, she answered freedom's call.
She never asked, "Dad, why me?" She fought and died for us all.

She accepted life's greatest challenge; she put her life right on the line.
Now she walks with the Lord in heaven.
Daddy's little soldier girl is doing fine.

(11-07-2003)

When a Soldier Cries

It's not often that that you'll see,
Tears come to a soldiers eyes.
When he holds his newborn baby in his arms.
When in his arms, a buddy dies.
Those are times, when unashamed,
you just might see a soldier cry.

When a young soldier says good-bye
You'll seldom ever see him cry.
His eyes are dry, but deep inside,
If you could hear his heart, you would hear it cry.
Away from home and love he must go,
To fight for reasons, he may not know.

The tears of joy, flow endlessly,
As home again to his love he'll be.
When Taps is played and our flag flies high
It's hard to hold back the tears of pride.

When he hears 'The Star Spangled Banner',
or 'America the Beautiful'
When he honors a fallen friend,
These are times when with head held high,
You just might see a soldier cry.

(7/10/2007)

22

THE RANGERS ARE BACK

DURING OUR DMOR ceremony in 2005, we were told that the 2nd Battalion of the 16th Infantry Regiment was going to be reactivated. This was great news to all of the Vietnam vets who were part of the 2nd Battalion 16th Infantry in our 16th Infantry Regimental Association. In January 2006, a contingent of us traveled down to Fort Riley once again—this time, to be a small part of history with the re-flagging of the 2nd of the 16th "Rangers." Several former officers of the 2nd of the 16th, along with WWII vet Bill Ryan and I, were on hand to witness this event. The Honorary Colonel of the Regiment, Jerry Griffin, presented several items of 2nd of the 16th memorabilia to the new Battalion Commander, LTC Ralph Kauzlarich, and his men. These included an Alpha Company 2nd of the 16th guide-on that was flown by Jerry Griffins Company in Vietnam. Now somewhat tattered and worn, it will be on display in the 2nd of the 16th Ranger's Headquarters at Fort Riley for all to see.

LTC Kauzlarich was a seasoned war veteran, having served in combat in Afghanistan. His task was to stand up a totally new battalion, train them, and take them to war in Iraq—a very difficult task, to say the least. I became good friends with "Colonel K," as he was known by his soldiers and friends. Most of the old soldiers were invited over to Colonel K's quarters, along with a large number of the soldiers from the new Battalion. We met his wife, Stephanie, and their three children, and had a great

2nd Battalion 16th Infantry reflagging ceremony, January 2006. Left to right: CSM Scott Smith, LTC Frank Zachar, Jerry Griffin (Honorary Colonel of the Regiment), LTC Ralph Kauzlarich, and CSM Michael McCoy. (Photo from the author's collection.)

time socializing with the officers and men of the newly reflagged 2nd Battalion 16th Infantry.

In February 2007, Colonel K and his soldiers were deployed as part of President Bush's "Surge." This was a plan to send over a large number of troops to help quell the violence in and around Baghdad. They were assigned to one of the worst areas for violence between the Sunnis and the Shiites. Their area of operation was just southeast of Baghdad at a forward operating base called Rustamiyah. To read more about that deployment, check out a book titled *The Good Soldiers*, by David Finkel. A tough year cost the Rangers fourteen men killed in action, and many soldiers were left with life-altering injuries from wounds. Most were killed by improvised explosive devices; in Vietnam, we just called them land mines. The Hodgies had perfected these devices to where they could be set off with a cell phone or other electronic devices.

During the first part of the War on Terror, the 16th Infantry consisted of just one battalion: the 1st Battalion, Iron Rangers. In 2004, at the BRO reunion in Chicago, we met a couple of guys from Charlie Company 1st of the 16th who had been on a Bradley fighting vehicle when it was hit with a rocket-propelled grenade. Lieutenant Lonnie Moore and Sergeant David Sterling were on the same vehicle. Lt. Moore lost a leg and Sgt. Sterling lost his right hand. Another Charlie Company soldier who had been wounded in another incident was with them in Chicago. His name was Joe Mosner, from St. Paul, Minnesota.

Janet and I had the good fortune to spend some time with Lonnie Moore when we visited the Cantigny Museum as part of the reunion. He was having some difficulty adjusting to his new prosthetic leg, but he did quite well. Lonnie went on to become very involved with Wounded Warrior programs throughout the country. He wanted to stay in the Army, but due to his prosthetic leg, he could not stay in the Infantry, so he took a medical retirement. In October, 2009, Captain (Ret.) Lonnie Moore was inducted into the 16th Infantry Regimental Association as a DMOR; one of the first of our modern-day warriors to be recognized.

Dave Sterling also ended up with a medical retirement. He chose to stay in the Fort Riley area and now works on-base, in range control. He builds targets and other things needed for the firing ranges. His drive, determination, and positive attitude are an inspiration to the young soldiers and civilian contractors that he works with. In July 2009, Dave Sterling was awarded a Silver Star by Major General Vincent Brooks for his actions on the day that he and Lieutenant Moore were injured, a well-deserved and long-awaited honor.

After the Iron Rangers returned from Iraq in 2004, Lt. Col. Frank Zachar took over the Command of the 1st Battalion 16th Infantry at Fort Riley. I first met Lt. Col. Zachar at the 1st Infantry Division reunion in D.C. in 2005. He was very helpful working with the Regimental Association during his command, many times having us over to his quarters on Fort Riley. During his command, the Iron Rangers would be deployed a second time, only this would be very different. Alpha Company was deployed to "the Horn of Africa" in March 2006. Bravo and Charlie companies would later be deployed to Iraq. Lt. Col. Zachar left Fort Riley in 2006 to go to the War College, and has since been promoted to full Colonel and has been assigned a regimental command in Germany.

Shortly after the return of the Charlie Company, 1st of the 16th "Wolfhounds" from their first deployment, a few old Bandidos got to talking about how nice it would be if Charlie Company 1st of the 16th would take back the name "Bandido Charlie." This would of course have to be approved by the current chain of command and men of Charlie Company 1st of the 16th. Phil Greenwell, Al Herrera, Doug Ludlow, Woody Goldberg, and a few others got in touch with Captain Michael Squires. He was the Company Commander for Charlie Company 1st of the 16th at the time. When Captain Squires heard the history of the Bandidos from Vietnam, he was very enthusiastic about changing the name of the Wolfhounds to the Bandidos.

This was eventually submitted to the Department of the Army, and as it stands now, "Bandido Charlie 1st of the 16th (Mech) Infantry" is the only company-sized unit with a name authorized by the Department of the Army.

The legacy that was brought to the new Bandidos by the Vietnam era Bandidos instilled a level of unit pride and esprit de corps that is hard to top. Under the leadership of Captain Michael Squires, the Bandidos soon learned that they were now part of something much bigger than themselves. They were writing their own chapter in the history of the 16th Infantry Regiment and the Big Red One. This created some problems for the Battalion Commander, as he now found himself with one company of hard-charging Bandidos, ready to lead the way, setting a standard that was difficult for others to replicate.

At the 16th Infantry Ball during DMOR week in 2005, an outsider would have thought that the Bandidos were the main body of the Regiment on that evening. The unit pride was busting at its seams. Lt. Col. Zacher stated at one time that as difficult as it was to control the hard-charging Bandidos, he wished that he had four companies of them instead of just one.

During 2005, Captain Squires transferred out and was replaced by his friend, Captain Scott Wence. Captain Squires moved on to become a part of Delta Force, and the Bandidos, now with Captain Wence and 1st Sgt. Chris Johnson in the lead, never missed a beat. They trained up and deployed to Iraq in September, 2007, as did the Bushmasters of Bravo Company, 1st of the 16th Infantry.

The Bandidos headquartered out of Al Asad and ran convoy escort with their Bradleys, Humvees, and other fighting vehicles. They built a building where they would assemble for mission briefings and debriefings, and named it after our First Sergeant from 'Nam, Alfredo Herrera. They called it Herrera Hall—quite an honor for our Top Sergeant.

The Bandidos in Iraq really did us all proud. They ran several missions every day, and never had a single KIA during their entire year in Iraq. It appeared that the Hodgies had gotten the word not to mess with the Bandidos. This didn't bode well for the other units that were providing convoy security in this AO, as the Hodgies would let the Bandidos pass and then hit the less organized troops from other units. It was kind of like the old surfer song by the Beach boys, "The bad boys know us and they leave us alone."

When the Bandidos came home from Iraq, a number of the old Bandidos decided to meet them for their homecoming. This was planned for late October. Several of the guys had mentioned that we should ride our motorcycles down there. When I left home at 7:00 a.m., the temperature was thirty-five degrees. I bundled up with a lot of warm clothes and headed south.

Four hours later, I pulled into a gas station in Sioux City, Iowa, to fill up. I got talking with a gal at the pumps and she was telling me that her brother had just recently deployed to Iraq. Seeing my Patriot Guard sticker on my windshield, she just had to say thanks. I went inside to the men's room and got out of some of my heavy clothes. When I got back out to my Harley, there was a twenty-dollar gas card laying on the seat and a little thank you note mentioning the Patriot Guard.

When I got to Manhattan, Kansas, I called a friend of mine, Richard Martinson. He was a Captain with Bravo Company, 1st of the 16th, and just recently returned from Iraq. He and his gal, Emily, had an apartment in Manhattan and had invited me to stay with them while I was down there. Richard had just taken command of the Commanding Generals Mounted Color Guard. Saturday afternoon, Richard took us for a tour of the Mounted Color Guard stables and shared with us some of the history of the Commanding General's Mounted Color Guard. We also toured the Custer Museum at Fort Riley.

On Saturday evening, I rode over to the American Legion Post in Manhatten and met up with several of the Bandidos, including First Sergeant Chris Johnson. He presented me with a Bandido challenge coin that he and Captain Scott Wence had made up while they were in Iraq. A bit later, I met up with Phil and Linda Greenwell, Doug and Catherine Ludlow, and Pete De-LaFuentes and his wife. We all served with Bandido Charlie Company in Vietnam together. We had a great time welcoming home our modern-day Bandidos.

On Sunday, Phil, Doug, Pete, and their ladies all left for home. However, having a special request from a friend to attend his promotion ceremony on Monday morning, I stayed over. On Sunday afternoon, I thought that I would get out of the apartment to let my two young friends have some time without the old guy hanging around, so I rode out to the post to see if I could find Lt. Col. Zachar's place. When I got close to the post, I stopped and unfurled my American flag and my Patriot Guard flag. As I rode around on post, they waved proudly behind my Harley. When I got to what looked like Lt. Col. Zachar's quarters, I parked the

Harley and was busy taking my helmet off and storing a few things in the saddle bags when I noticed a van had pulled up right behind me. Out pops this good looking little blond gal. She came up to me and asked if I was with the Patriot Guard.

She had seen my flag and had put two and two together. I told her that I was a member of the Patriot Guard and she commenced to tell me that her husband had just recently deployed to Iraq. She said that before he left, he had been down at Fort Benning, Georgia, and there had been a funeral for a soldier who was killed in Iraq. There were a couple hundred Patriot Guard Riders there to honor that soldier. Her husband was very impressed and told her all about it.

Before she left, she looked at me with those pretty little blue eyes filled with tears and asked me if she could give me a hug. No mission too difficult, no sacrifice too great, duty first. I gave her a fatherly hug and sent her on her way.

After that, I walked across the street where I found Frankie and Wolfie, the Zachar boys, playing out back. They went in and got their dad, and he invited me in. Michelle had just taken some fresh homemade bread out and offered me a slice. It reminded me of what my mother and grandmother used to make. It was awesome. We visited for an hour or so and then they had to get going, as Frank was taking the boys out fishing.

On Monday morning, I packed up my bag, said goodbye to Richard and Emily, thanked them for their hospitality, and headed out to Camp Funston for the promotion ceremony of my friend, Moses Scheinfeld. He was being promoted to the rank of Major that morning and having asked me to be present, how could I not be there to see him honored in this way? Woody Goldberg, who was one of my company commanders over in Vietnam, was also there to share the occasion. The three of us had our picture taken out front of Battalion HQ before I had to leave.

I left Fort Riley around 11:30 a.m. and arrived home, 585 miles later, at 9:15 p.m. Needless to say, I didn't ride much the following week.

Major Moses Scheinfeld, Woody Goldberg, and Ron Mackedanz at
Camp Funston (Fort Riley, KS), October 2008.
(Photo courtesy of Moses Scheinfeld.)

23

REUNIONS AND DMOR WEEK

IN 1983, I was working for Production Credit Association out of Olivia. Over the past fourteen years or so, I had not had much contact with any of the guys who had been in 'Nam with me. Then one day, I got a letter from David Komes's wife, Dianna. She said that they, along with Dennis Silvia, were putting together a small reunion out in Anderson, Indiana. They wanted to know if we would come.

Janet and I talked about it and we thought that it might be good to see some of the guys and meet their families. I was down in Minneapolis the week before the reunion for some Ag lending seminars, so on Thursday, Janet drove down with the kids and we headed east on our adventure.

We were booked into the Holiday Inn in Anderson, Indiana, and they treated us like royalty. Those attending were David and Dianna Komes and their two boys, Jeff and Calvin; David and Roseanne Jeffrey; Jerry Hartman; Gene and Jeanie Zemple; Norm and Sharon Hardin; Dennis Silvia; Vernon Feeler; and Janet and me, along with our two daughters, Brenda and Dawna. There were a few others, but once again, I don't recall their names.

I had taken a slide projector along, as well as about one hundred slides from Vietnam. We showed them one night in one of the rooms. I recall that a couple of the wives thanked me. They had never seen any pictures from there and didn't have a clue what their husbands had done. Now they knew.

That night, the guys all went down by the pool, had a few beers, and just talked about shared experiences. Many of us were in the same ambushes and firefights together, but it's amazing how each of us remembered things a little bit differently about each of them.

We laughed, told jokes, and listened to each other tell stories about the others they were with. At one time, two of the guys were lying on the pool deck holding their bellies and almost crying from laughing so hard. Finally the management came out and asked us to take our party inside. Some of their guests didn't seem to be as appreciative of our group as the management was.

Of course, when we parted company on Sunday, we all swore that we would stay in touch. With a few exceptions, that didn't happen. Dave Jeffreys asked us to stop at their home in Marion, Indiana, on our way home, so after saying our goodbyes, we followed them north. After visiting for a little while, Dave went out and returned with an old SKS rifle that he had brought back from 'Nam. It was something that he had put away and rarely ever brought out. He shared with me the circumstances by which he acquired the rifle and then we went and put it away again. But that's his story to tell, not mine. Over the next few years, we managed to stay in touch with the Komes' and the Hardins. Other than that, the others just seemed to drift away again.

Every year for the past eight years, my wife Janet and I have been attending the 1st Infantry Division Reunions: New Orleans in 2002; Reno, Nevada, in 2003; Chicago in 2004; Washington, D.C., in 2005; Phoenix in 2006; St. Louis in 2007; Colorado Springs in 2008; and Dearborn in 2009.

In New Orleans, we had just five of us there, but the following year in Reno, we had twenty-two Bandidos and their guests at the reunion. Each year since then has held something special. In Phoenix, I finally got the chance to meet Ken Costich. He was Bandido Charlie Six during the spring and part of the summer of 1969. I drove his command track during that time.

We have also made several trips to Fort Riley for the 16th Infantry Regiment Distinguished Member of the Regiment week and other events. These events are always a highlight for me. At Fort Riley, we have the opportunity to visit with the active duty soldiers of today's all-volunteer Army. They are without a doubt the best, most highly trained soldiers to be found anywhere in the military. It is always interesting to go out and watch the soldiers going through their training missions.

A couple of years back, some of us old war dogs were given the opportunity to take up positions on four different Humvees. The lead unit and the rear unit each had a fifty-caliber machine gun. The two in the middle had M-240 machine guns. We would be taking part in a simulated ambush on the way out to the training area. I jumped on the fifty on the rear unit. For me, it was kind of a metal test, or gut check. I had to see how I would react when the ambush was blown. My last act in combat was manning the fifty-caliber after the command track that I was driving had been disabled by a rocket-propelled grenade. My gunner and First Sergeant were both wounded and we had no one on our fifty, so I took over and started firing at the NVA soldiers who were dug in a mere twenty yards in front of us. As things happened, I didn't last very long up there. They took me off the fifty with another rocket-propelled grenade. So getting back in the saddle, even in a simulated situation, was something that I felt I had to do.

When the IED went off beside one of the Humvees in our column, Hodgies started appearing with RPGs and AK-47s, shooting at us from both sides. Covering the rear of our column, I had a good field of fire and lit up those Hodgies pretty well. It felt good. I was able to react the way that is needed in combat and I was pleased with that.

Once we arrived at our destination, we were able to fire several different weapons, including the M-240 Squad automatic weapon, the M-4, and a couple foreign weapons. This is always interesting. Some of the wives also came along out and they got a rush out of shooting things up, just like the big boys.

The year that I was inducted as a DMOR, we went into a room that was set up with several machine guns, including the fifty-caliber machine gun, also known as the Ma Deuce. My daughter, Dawna, was with me and we had soldiers who were assisting us with firing the different weapons. They were falling all over themselves, trying to impress Dawna with their knowledge and abilities with the different weapons. This was the year that the 1st Battalion was hosting the DMOR event. At one point, I was with LTC Frank Zacher as we were working our way up to the room where the simulators were set up. We came to a door that was locked and we were certain that it led to the room that we were looking for. When we received no reply after banging on the door, LTC Zacher told me to stand back; he was getting ready to kick the door in when we heard movement on the other side. Luckily someone opened it up, saving us from making a forced entry.

During the DMOR week, we were given the royal treatment on post. The young soldiers enjoyed hearing us tell about our time in combat, especially hearing the stories of the WWII veterans who make the trip with us each year. We have several D-Day veterans who actually made the assault on Omaha Beach on June 6, 1944: Bill Ryan, Ray Lambert, Harley Reynolds, Steve Kellman, Arthur Schintzel, Joseph Argenzio, and Charles Shay. These guys have been the backbone of the 16th Infantry Regiment Association for many years. Tales of their time during "The Big War" never ceases to entertain the many young active duty soldiers, as well as a few of us old Vietnam vets.

In December 2005, I received a phone call from Debbie Hatterman, Curtis's wife. Curtis had died suddenly on December 14. One of his last wishes was to have a motorcycle escort for his funeral. Curtis had done so much for the Bandidos, putting together a web site and maintaining contact with several of the 9th Division Bandidos. We had become great friends over the past few years, helping each other with all sorts of things, but mainly just being friends.

Living in Minnesota, I had put my Harley in storage with the local Harley shop. However, when Debbie called, I didn't hesitate. I told her that I would be there. I called the owner of Apol's Harley shop in Raymond, Minnesota, told him what had happened, and that I needed my Harley.

I drove over that very afternoon, we loaded my Harley in the back of my pickup, and away I went. I drove in snow all the way through Minnesota, Iowa, Nebraska, and Kansas. When I got about thirty miles north of Enid, Oklahoma, I finally ran out of the snow.

The morning of the funeral it was twenty-five degrees out, but the roads were clear and dry, so I unloaded the Harley and rode over to the funeral home. Some of the guys from the local Vietnam Veteran's of America chapter were supposed to ride, but I guess that it was a little too chilly for the boys down south. Either that or they had more common sense than I did. Finally, one of their guys came riding up on his Goldwing. He and I would lead the hearse over to the cemetery.

In June 2006, the 5th Battalion 60th Infantry Association held their biennial reunion in St. Louis. After meeting Wendy Winslow, Lee Alley, Chester Jahn, and several other Bandidos from the 5th of the 60th, I decided to accept the invitation to come down. They run a great reunion. My wife and I were treated well and felt like we belonged. They do a special memorial each time they have a reunion and pay tribute to the buddies that they have lost since the last reunion. Special tribute was paid to Curtis Hatterman for all the effort he had put into bringing the Battalion back together again.

Ron Mackedanz on the Harley, with Earl Massey (second from the left) and members of the VVA chapter in Enid, Oklahoma, for Curtis Hatterman's funeral. December 19, 2005.
(Photo from the author's collection.)

Members of Bandido Charlie Company 5th Battalion 60th Infantry and Ron Mackedanz, a Bandido from the 1st of the 16th (mech. Inf.). Holding the flag: Alan Kisling. Front row, left to right: Jackson Davis, Robert "Doc" Todd, Wayne Parrish, Charlie Taylor, Wendy Winslow, Ron Mackedanz, Lee Alley. Back row: Ron Mayville, Gary Bobbit, Clemmie Jenkins, unknown, John Holhman and James Murphy (2006 at St. Louis).
(Photo from the author's collection.)

Jon Lindstrand with a Montagnard crossbow that he brought for our
mini-reunion in August 2007.
(Photo from the author's collection.)

Ron Mackedanz, David Komes, Jerry Harman, Gene Zemple, and Dave Jeffrey, August 2007 at Ron's place in Minnesota.
(Photo from the author's collection.)

Gene and Jeanie Zemple, Ron and Janet Mackedanz, Dave and Roseanne Jeffrey, David and Dianna Komes, and Jerry and Sue Hartman at Ron's place in Minnesota, August 2007.
(Photo from the author's collection.)

24

THE PATRIOT GUARD

IN 2005, A GROUP OF American Legion Riders, in response to demonstrations by radical members of the Westboro Baptist Church out of Topeka, Kansas, rode their motorcycles to the funeral of a young soldier killed in Iraq. The protesters, hiding behind the First Amendment of our Constitution, shouted and waved signs that said, "Thank God for dead soldiers," and "Your son deserved to die," and other horrible things that demean our servicemen and women who have sacrificed their lives for our rights to live free.

From this action, the Patriot Guard was born. Many states passed laws restricting the protesters' distance to the family of the fallen. The uninvited guests (they became known to the Patriot Guard as "UGs") were required to contact the law enforcement from the area and let them know that they intended to show up. As time went along, it seemed that the UGs would notify the authorities of their intentions to show up, just to get people on edge. Often, they wouldn't show.

The Patriot Guard is made up of people from all walks of life. Most ride motorcycles, a large number are veterans, and many are people who just want to show respect, honor, and dignity to the families of the fallen that they deserve.

No confrontations with protesters are allowed. That's where law enforcement comes in. If there is a problem, the PGR will turn their backs to the protesters, blocking them out from the sight of the family during their time of mourning. The Patriot

Guard is active in every state in the USA; Minnesota has over 5,600 members. Not to be confused with a motorcycle club, the Patriot Guard is not a club. It is just a group of like-minded people riding for a cause that they believe in: to be supportive of our service members and their families.

I first became aware of the Patriot Guard back in the spring of 2006. Then in June 2006, a young soldier from our area was killed in Iraq, and several others were wounded. Brent Koch from Morton, Minnesota, was the first of many to whom I would pay tribute while standing the flag line with the Minnesota Patriot Guard Riders. Not knowing much about it, I rode the seventy miles to the south central Minnesota town of Morgan where the funeral was being held. One of the Patriot Guard members directed me to a van and a gal with extra flags for those of us who did not have one. Standing in the flag line prior to the funeral was quite moving. During the funeral, we stood down for a short time to get a drink of water and meet other members. When the services were over, they brought the casket out with a full military escort. Prior to loading the casket into the hearse, three white doves were released. Two of them took right off. The third one made a small circle and returned to perch on the roof to the entrance of the school where the casket waited to be loaded in the hearse. For many of us, this was a small sign of a higher power.

Many of the Patriot Guard riders accompanied the family from Morgan down to Trimont, Minnesota, for internment. I was not able to make the trip, but it is my understanding that there were over one hundred motorcycles with the "Stars and Stripes" proudly flying. At many places along the route, people stood with flags, showing their support and respect for a young soldier who gave his life for the freedom of others.

Just a couple of weeks later, west central Minnesota suffered another casualty in the War on Terror. On June 29, 2006, nineteen-year-old Kyle Miller from Bird Island and Willmar was killed in action. Kyle's funeral, the second one that I would attend as part of the MN Patriot Guard, was held in Willmar at the Civic

Center. Over one hundred and fifty motorcycles were on hand, with over two hundred members standing a flag line in front of the Civic Center. Fortunately, no protesters showed up. After the services, we escorted the family with a mile-long line of motorcycles over to Fairview Cemetery for the internment. Kyle was buried in the area of the cemetery known as Soldier's Rest, also known by some as the Circle of Honor.

The remainder of 2006 was filled with missions throughout the states of Minnesota, Wisconsin, and South and North Dakota. Whenever I could, I would ride out to pay tribute to these fallen servicemen and women. On November 1, 2006, about twenty Patriot Guard riders met in Morris, Minnesota, to ride over for the funeral services of SSG Kevin Witte, who was killed on October 20, 2006, in Baghdad, Iraq. The temperature that morning was twenty-five degrees and the wind was blowing strong out of the northwest. When we arrived in Beardsley, we were asked to ride over to Browns Valley to meet and escort the hearse and the family back over to the church at Beardsley. As we waited in a rest area near the South Dakota border, we could see a snow squall building just over the border in South Dakota. None of us were eager to ride in a snow storm. Kevin Witte's grandfather came out and greeted each of us, thanking us for being there.

As the hearse pulled into the rest area, the snow started. Luckily, it didn't last but a few minutes. We took off for Beardsley, two-by-two in front of the hearse. When we came around the corner near the church in Beardsley, it was difficult not to choke up. There, lining the sidewalks in front of the church, with windchills down around zero degrees, were forty Patriot Guard members, all with flags flying high and proud. An entire busload had made the trip out from the Metro area. SSG Witte was buried at Arlington National Cemetery later in November.

A week or so later, we had an Honor Mission for a WWII veteran down in Gaylord, Minnesota. The weather was somewhat warmer, so I decided to ride. Lori and Andy Musolf were the ride captains for the Willmar sector of the Patriot Guard. Lori drove down that day, and before the day was over, she had me talked into joining the leadership team as an assistant ride captain. I told her that I would do it until they could find someone else. Famous last words.

2007 turned out to be a busy year for the Patriot Guard. Along with the funeral missions, we also had the 34th Infantry Red Bulls returning from a sixteen-month deployment to Iraq. In April, we received word that another local soldier had been killed. Joshua Schmit of Willmar was killed by a roadside bomb just a week or so short of his return home. Once again, we staged at the Willmar Senior High school for the short ride over to the Civic Center. Andy and Lori organized the mission and Mike Remarke (a Marine) and I assisted. We had over one hundred twenty-five motorcycles and approximately two hundred members in the flag line. Many people coming across the overpass told us how breathtaking the flag line was. As veterans, Mike and I were asked to lead the procession from the Civic Center to the cemetery. This was quite an honor. Josh was buried next to Kyle Miller at Soldier's Rest in Willmar.

During the summer of 2007, we had the great fortune to escort several bus loads of Red Bulls home to Camp Ripley, Hutchinson, New Ulm, and several other Minnesota communities. Twice, we met buses in Clearwater, and escorted them up to Camp Ripley. Our route took us through Little Falls, where the streets were lined with little kids, old folks, and everyone in between, waving flags and hollering "Welcome Home!" to the returning troops. Riding onto Camp Ripley with the buses loaded with soldiers coming home was an awesome experience.

Andy and Lori Musolf and I rode down to Woodbury to ride escort with six other Patriot Guard members. Three busloads of 34th Infantry Red Bulls were returning to Hutchinson, which happens to be my hometown. We met the buses at Woodbury and escorted them around the Metro area on I-494. When we got around to the west side of Minneapolis, three state troopers swooped down in front of us and led us through the entire west metro. Every intersection had police cars halting traffic so that our convoy could proceed without stopping for traffic lights. Once out of the metro, we were on our own until we got to the McLeod County line where we were once again met by local law enforcement. They led the way to and through Hutchinson. Just on the east side of Hutchinson, we stopped and picked up some of the Red Bulls who had come home earlier, so that they could jump in with their motorcycles and lead their buddies home.

As we rode down the main street of Hutchinson, there were a couple thousand people lining the streets. I felt like it was my own welcome home. The feeling of being a part of this is indescribable.

Once the troops unloaded and had their welcome home ceremony, they were dismissed to their families. I was asked if I would lead a group of seven soldiers from Glencoe home. We had about a dozen motorcycles in that escort, along with law enforcement from Glencoe and McLeod County.

One of the highlights of the summer was being asked to escort three busloads of Red Bulls on a leg of their trip home to Bemidji and Crookston, Minnesota. Our part of the escort involved intercepting them at Brandon, on I-94, just west of Alexandria. After swooping down the on-ramp with two other Patriot Guard members, I glanced back over my shoulder. Realizing that I had over one hundred young soldiers behind me, and that I was privileged to be a part of bringing them home to their families, I felt like every button on my shirt was going to pop. The pride in being a part of this was huge. Once we got up to Barnesville, where the next escort group was to take over, I parked my Harley and went over to the waiting bus. Then I shook hands with and welcomed home every one of the soldiers who had their window open. Later I told Alan Peterson (one of the other escorts) that I had just given those guys something that I never got: A welcome home.

In January 2008, we received word that a soldier from Granite Falls had been killed in Afghanistan. Matthew Kahler was serving with the 173rd Airborne. He was killed during combat operations on January 26, 2008. The Patriot Guard Riders from Minnesota were asked to participate in the three-phased mission honoring SSG Matthew Kahler. On Wednesday, February 6, 2008, more than thirty Patriot Guard members were on hand to meet the chartered plane bringing the body of Matthew Kahler home. The family was all at the Willmar Municipal Airport waiting for their soldier. As ride captain in charge of this mission, I was asked to bring six of our members out on the tarmac to provide a squad of prior service members to greet the casket and the escort. We stood there, at attention, as the plane crew prepared the casket for off loading. Six members of the military stood ready to accompany the body to the waiting hearse.

As we waited for them to carry the casket over to the hearse, we stood off to the side as the family stoically stood facing a stiff northwest wind. Matthew's little four-year-old daughter, Allison, held onto her mother's hand and danced impatiently. I couldn't help but think of all the questions that were going through her little mind. Once the hearse was loaded and the family, along with many law enforcement and emergency vehicles, were lined up, the Patriot Guard lined both sides of the road leaving the airport. Flags were flying in the wind and veterans were saluting our fallen hero as they left for the forty mile trip to Granite Falls.

On Friday evening, February 8, with temperatures down around zero and a stiff wind blowing twenty miles per hour, over ninety members of the Patriot Guard stood in honor of Matthew Kahler. The visitation was held at the Granite Falls Lutheran Church in Granite Falls. Many of the Patriot Guard Riders stayed the night in Granite Falls or the neighboring town of Montevideo. Hundreds of people from all across the country attended the visitation.

The morning of Saturday, February 9, dawned extremely cold. A lot of folks, including some members of the Patriot Guard, were forced to turn around due to near-blizzard conditions. Still, we had around one hundred Patriot Guard members there for the funeral. We stood a flag line outside of the church as family and friends of the Kahler's made their way inside for the service. During the service, some ladies from the church invited us into a small house near the church that was used for Sunday school classes. There, we were able to warm up a bit with coffee and cookies. Shortly before the service ended, we formed our flag line outside of the church and surrounded the hearse as the casket was brought out. Then about thirty-five of us boarded a school bus and headed out to the cemetery on the south side of the Minnesota River, near the Prairie's Edge Casino.

As we sat at the cemetery on the bus, the wind picked up more and more. By the time the family and the hearse arrived, the temperature had dropped to fifteen degrees below zero and the winds were whipping around twenty miles per hour. It was brutal out there. When we saw the buses with the family coming, we grabbed our gear, unfurled our flags, and set our flag line. The honor guard squad, made up of active duty soldiers, wore their dress Greens and no overcoats. From my position in the flag line, I could see that they were freezing. As soon as the rifle salute was finished, one of the members of the rifle squad broke ranks and headed for the van. She appeared to be on the verge of hypothermia.

With almost a foot of snow on the ground and the temps as they were, it was not a place for people who were not dressed for the weather. I especially remember a lady with no boots, just a pair of dress shoes, standing there in the snow, shivering and shaking. One of our members, who we all call Scotty, was wearing a huge wolf skin trapper's cap. Seeing the lady standing in the snow with street shoes, Scotty handed his flag to another Patriot Guard member, ran through the snow and placed his cap down for the lady to stand on. Who says chivalry is dead?

As the internment services progressed, the Patriot Guard stood fast to their flag line. The last thing that the family saw as they left the cemetery was a line of flags with Patriot Guard members standing guard over their soldier. Once the family had left, we furled our flags and headed for the bus. Many of our group made our way over to Matthew's gravesite to salute and pay our last respects.

Members of the Minnesota Patriot Guard standing in honor of
SSG Matthew Kahler, February 9, 2008.
(Photo from the author's collection.)

The American Legion Club in Granite Falls had invited the Patriot Guard members over for hot drinks and sandwiches after the funeral. Boy! Were we ready for that! It felt good to get into someplace warm and shed a few layers. A couple of years have passed since Matthew's death. His father, Ron Kahler, has become a close friend over the past few years.

In the summer of 2009, a friend of mine, Jeff Seeber, also known as "Sailor Doc," put together a "Tribute to the Fallen." Just about every weekend, he and his wife, Candice, would drive hundreds of miles, visiting the gravesites of our fallen soldiers from all over Minnesota. Sailor Doc was a Navy Corpsman who served with a Marine unit in Vietnam. He is one of the most dedicated guys that I know when it comes to our current servicemen and women.

When I found out that Doc was planning a weekend run out through west central Minnesota, I volunteered to help coordinate the trip. Doc and his group had purchased patriotic floral arrangements for each gravesite that we visited that weekend. The couple of weeks prior to our run, I visited the local law enforcement in each of the towns that we would be going through and arranged road guard protection for our group of riders that would be accompanying us.

The day started out for us in Litchfield, Minnesota, where we staged about twenty motorcycles and six cars. From there, we headed west to Kandiyohi, where we visited the gravesite of Ryan Cain. As we pulled up to the cemetery, there were about fifty family members and friends of the Cains there. Janet and I did the honors there and Doc said a few words in tribute to Ryan Cain, in honor of his service.

From there, we headed over to Willmar and paid tribute to Kyle Miller and Joshua Schmit. Along with our group and a few family members, the local NG unit had sent a detail over to take part in the tribute. Both Kyle and Josh had been killed in Iraq by IED explosions. Upon leaving Willmar, we had a sixty-mile ride west, out to Madison, Minnesota. In May 2007, an Iraq War veteran, Brian Skold, had been dealing with PTSD and had not received the treatment that he needed. He ended up getting into a confrontation with law enforcement and was killed. I was out in California at the time. I know that it's not very likely, but I've always felt like that if I'd been home, that I might have been able to somehow intervene and talk Brian down. It's something that we'll never know. When we got to the cemetery in Madison, once again, family members joined in for our tribute to Brian. They were deeply moved by our presence there. Many other veterans, Patriot Guard members and I believe that even though some of these young people took their own lives, they are still casualties of the War.

Our next stop was just fifteen miles away in Dawson. On August 1, 2008, twenty-four-year-old David Staab, suffering from PTSD after a year in Iraq, took his life. I was out in Wisconsin when I received word from Alan Peterson, the Marshall sector ride captain. It was Sunday evening when Alan called me, and the funeral was being planned for Tuesday, so Monday morning I got on my Harley and rode out to Dawson to meet with the funeral director. We had been asked by the family to be present for David's wake and funeral. The wake was Monday evening and due to such a short notice, we only had six Patriot Guard members there standing a flag line outside of the funeral home.

When Alan Peterson arrived, he and I went inside to offer our condolences to David's folks. His mom was standing in front of me and his dad was standing in front of Alan. After saying what we could, Cindy and Mike thanked us for being there. I could see that Mike was really struggling, so I just stepped over and put my arms around him and held him as he sobbed. What else could I do? There are no words that you can offer at a time like that. Since then, whenever anyone asks me why we do what we do, I simply tell them, "Until you have held the grieving parent or spouse of a fallen soldier in your arms while they cried their tears of grief, you will never fully understand it."

Later that evening, one of David Staab's uncles came out and stood squarely in front of me. He was a big man, towering over me. He looked me in the eye, and I wasn't sure if this was good or not. Then he offered his hand and said, "You have no idea what you have done for this family tonight." With just a handful of Patriot Guard members standing out in front of the funeral home, it had showed David's family that people cared.

When I called the Staab's in the summer of 2009 and asked if it would be okay with them if we included David in our "Tribute to the Fallen," they were very happy about it. Cindy Staab asked me if they could provide refreshments for our group or something. We were going to be on a very tight schedule so I told her that a cooler full of ice water would be great. When we arrived at the cemetery that afternoon, they had a couple of tables set up with sandwiches, chips, bars, and cold drinks. We did our tribute to David and then went to the lunch that was being provided for us. Before we left, David's eleven-year-old niece, Brook, read a poem that one of her teachers had helped her write. There wasn't a dry eye in the place by the time she finished.

Next stop: Granite Falls, for a tribute to SSG Matthew Kahler. Matthew's father and stepmother were riding with us that day. As we pulled into town, I realized that I didn't need to be in the lead. I asked the guy next to me to drop back and have Ron and his wife come up and take the lead going out to the cemetery. Matthew is buried on the south side of the Minnesota River bluffs overlooking the river and the city of Granite Falls. It is an area that is rich with Native American history.

Matthew's widow, Vicki Kahler, and daughter, Allison, were there, as were his mother, Colleen, and a few other family members.

Our last stop of the day was near the little blink-your-eye-and-you-missed-it town of Green Valley, Minnesota. This was the final resting place of Lt. Jason Timmerman. Jason was killed in February 2005, along with two other men from the Montevideo Guard unit. Jesse Lhotka, David Day, and Jason Timmerman all died in an IED explosion. One of our assistant ride captains from the Marshall sector, Chris Dunsmore, served in Iraq with them at the time they were killed. Needless to say, Chris took it pretty hard. When "Tribute to the Fallen" came

Matthew, Allison, and Vicki Kahler, February 2007.
(Photo courtesy of Vicki Kahler.)

SFC Matthew Kahler, KIA Afghanistan January 26, 2008.
SSG Troy Ezernak, KIA October 9, 2005.
(Photo courtesy of Ron Kahler.)

around, Chris was selected to place the floral arrangement at each of their gravesites.

When we rode into the cemetery at Green Valley, there were a large number of family members and friends there to greet us. Chris did the honors, Jeff Seeber said his words of tribute, and after that we all visited with the family before heading for Marshall where we would spend the night.

On Sunday morning, with rain coming down, Alan Peterson and I rode ahead to Lake Benton to provide road guard for the rest of the group. Fortunately, the rain ceased. We then made our way to Edgerton, Trimont, and Welcome, Minnesota, to pay tribute to four more fallen soldiers. By the time I had arrived home, I had ridden over five hundred miles and never left the state.

The Patriot Guard is one of the greatest groups of people that I have ever been associated with. I have given a lot to the Patriot Guard, but I have received way more than I have given. This is a group of people whose only desire is to show honor, dignity, and respect to our servicemen and women and their families.

25

DRAGON WEEK

IN MAY 2009, JANET AND I attended the wedding of our good friend and past State Ride Captain for the Minnesota Patriot Guard. The first week in May, Monica Mead married Butch Wesley, a Vietnam veteran. Butch lost a leg in 'Nam, and he has been active in motorcycle riding for many years. They got married at the local VFW club surrounded by hundreds of their biker friends.

A few days later, Mike LaBelle and I took a trip to Fort Riley, Kansas, to see friends of ours down there. Mike had been working with a group of people in Minnesota called Vets4Vets. They have been reaching out to Iraq and Afghan vets who have been having a rough time since returning from their deployments. With the large number of suicides that have been happening, a group of Vietnam Vets have been working to organize and reach out to these service men and women, whether they are still in the military or not.

Mike had a few contacts at Fort Riley that he wanted to meet with, and with me knowing my way around Fort Riley, it appeared to be a good time for a road trip. We had been looking for a good reason to ride our Harleys somewhere and this was it. We ended up staying with a First Sergeant friend of Mike's who lived off-post. The first day there, Mike and I went to go out on-post. To get on-post with motorcycles, the owner needs current registration, proof of insurance, a high visibility vest, boots, long pants, long sleeve shirt or jacket, and a helmet. This, along with proof of having taken an approved motorcycle safety class, might give someone a shot at it. A military I.D. by at least one person in the party is also required in most cases. Turns out, Mike couldn't find his current registration. We went over to the MP station to see if Mike could have his wife fax a copy of his registration down. In the process, lo and behold, Mike finally located the required document packed in his saddle bags.

We went over to the Black Hawk area and met with Mike's buddy, Rick. He showed us around his AO and then we went off-post to a Korean restaurant to meet a buddy of Rick's for lunch.

After lunch, we rode over to Camp Funston to visit the Iron Rangers of the 1st Battalion, 16th Infantry. We walked in and were immediately greeted by CSM David Kuhnert, the new Command Sergeant Major. Then Lt. Col. Bryan Luke came out to meet us. He invited us into his office where we visited for a time. Lt. Col. Luke's combat web gear, known as battle-rattle, was sitting on a chair near the door. I asked him if Mike could try it on so he could see how heavy it was compared with the flak vests that we had worn in Vietnam. The 1st Battalion was just starting to switch from training Iraqi security forces back to a combat arms battalion.

As a matter of protocol, I asked Lt. Col. Luke if we could go over and visit some of the company areas. We started out with Company C, also known as Bandido Charlie Company, where Company Commander Captain Wes Cheney welcomed us in. During the training assignment the battalion consisted of ten or twelve training companies of ten to fifteen men. Each company was made up of one officer and all the rest were NCOs. Their task was to train Iraqi National Police and military to take over responsibility of security in Iraq.

The Bandidos of Charlie Company had just recently started receiving new soldiers to build back up to normal strength. I asked Captain Cheney if I could address his group of new men, to which he agreed. I greeted the men and shared with them some of the lore of the Vietnam Bandidos. I presented them each with a Bandido Charlie pin, a copy of my booklet "Straight from the Gut," and a few other things. Letting new recruits see that they are part of something much bigger than themselves is always rewarding. Before leaving the battalion area, we stopped at the Alpha, Bravo, and Delta Company areas. Most were vacant or had only a couple of guys on duty.

Later that day, I called CSM Hutchison over at the 2nd of the 16th Rangers HQs. He told me that they were just wrapping up the 4th Brigade Dragon Week. This is a week of strenuous competition between all the units in the 4th Brigade Combat Team. He insisted that we come over the next day to join them for lunch and the awards presentation. Of course we accepted the invitation.

The next morning when Mike and I rode over there, we went directly over to Battalion HQ. As it turned out, Lt. Col. Kreis and CSM Hutchison were both down on the training field. We decided to head over there. No sooner had we got out the door heading for our Harleys, when there came Lt. Col. Kreis and CSM Hutchison. We were warmly greeted by them and escorted back to Battalion HQ. Once there, we took care of a little business, picking up our tickets for the 1st Infantry Division's Infantry Ball. Then Lt. Col. Kreis presented us each with a 2nd of the 16th Rangers pin. Knowing that they had some things to take care of before the awards presentation, Mike and I excused ourselves so that we wouldn't be in the way and promised to meet them for the picnic dinner that was being held prior to the awards presentation.

We headed over to the picnic area and hung with some of the soldiers from the 2nd of the 16th Rangers and some of the other units. Then Kelly Kreis, the Lt. Colonel's wife, showed up and asked me and Mike to join her for lunch. Of course, we accepted. I mean, how often does the Battalion Commander's wife offer to buy you lunch? Lt. Col. Kreis and CSM Hutchison joined us a few minutes later. As we were just finishing our lunch, the Kansas winds came up and blew over one of the tents that were set up for the lunch. A dozen or so soldiers soon had the problem taken care of.

After lunch, we headed over to the parade field where the troops were all assembled for the awards presentations. Many of the 2nd of the 16th Rangers received individual and team awards. Then the time came that we had all been waiting for: The presentation of the 4th Brigade Dragon Week first place Battalion trophy. Anticipation ran high; the Rangers had won most of the events in which they had participated, and in some cases, teams within the 2nd of the 16th Rangers were competing with each other for top honors. When the first place trophy was presented to the 2nd of the 16th Rangers, the roar from the Rangers was loud and clear. LTC Kreis, who stands well over six feet tall, proudly held the trophy up for all to see. It was great to be a guest of the 2nd of the 16th Rangers at this time and to share the victory with them.

The last night of our stay, we were honored to be a part of the 1st Infantry Division's Infantry Ball.

Ron Mackedanz and LTC Paul Kreis (Ranger Six) with 4th BCT Dragon Week trophy, May 2009.
(Photo from the author's collection.)

Ron Mackedanz with the 2nd Battalion, 16th Infantry soldiers who competed with the 4th Brigade Dragon Week competition, May 2009. (Photo from the author's collection.)

Mike LaBelle had never seen the likes of this evening. We had asked our friend, Rick, from the 3rd of the 1st "Nightmares," to attend the Ball with us. Even though he was not Infantry, he came and met some of his higher chain of command there. When asked what he was doing at an Infantry Ball, he promptly replied, "Sir, when I joined the Army, it was one war, one fight," to which the Colonel replied, "Good answer, First Sergeant."

During the Ball, CSM (Ret.) Bill Ryan was on hand to present flowers to the wives of the officers at the head table. Bill is always on hand to see to it that the ladies are recognized by the 16th Infantry Regiment. I had the pleasure of meeting the new 1st Infantry Division Commanding General, Major General Vincent Brooks, and his lovely wife, Carol. In the few minutes that I had to talk with them, I got the feeling that the Big Red One was in very capable hands. The main speaker for the evening was a Lieutenant General by the name of Stanley McChrystal. Seeing that I don't normally hang out with Colonels and Generals, I had not heard of General McChrystal. I asked MG Brooks if he would introduce me to the General. He did so and we had a very nice visit for a few minutes. Can you imagine my surprise when, a few days after I got home, I opened up the local newspaper and saw that General Stanley McChrystal had just been appointed the Commander of all U.S. forces in Afghanistan?

After the banquet meal, General McChrystal gave a talk to the soldiers and their guests, and I must say that it was one of the most entertaining speeches that I have ever heard a General make. It was light and at some points even humorous. He is definitely a leader who knows how to make his men feel at ease and still maintain a Command presence.

As we were sitting around visiting after the meal, Mike and Rick had gone out for a cigarette. I was just talking with a couple of guys when Mike came back in with a young sergeant from Bandido Charlie. I had been the editor of the 16th Infantry Newsletter for several years, and had somehow attained somewhat of a celebrity status with some of the young, very impressionable soldiers. It was almost embarrassing, the fuss that this young sergeant made when Mike told him that he was with Bandido Mack. I still laugh to think of it. Hell, I'm just one of the guys. After that little incident, Mike started giving me crap about me giving him my autograph. I told him to go fly a kite, but I may have used some other verbiage.

Later that evening, I went out to find Mike and Rick talking with a young captain and his lady friend. She was quite attractive and dressed to the nines. She said that she was from California and worked for one of the major TV news stations. Somehow or another the conversation got around to "winning the hearts and minds" of the Vietnamese population. When she asked me about it, I told her that we would do everything possible to show them that we were the good guys. If that didn't work, we'd just shoot 'em. I don't even know where that comment came from, but it certainly made an impact on her. Her eyes got big and she didn't know how to respond. There was not any truth to the "we'd just shoot 'em" part of that, but it sounded good at the time.

Rick and Mike were both standing there drinking a beer, and I thought Rick was going to choke on his. Later he said to me, "That was a classic." One has to have served in combat to see the humor in that.

1st Sgt. Rick Wilhelmy, Ron Mackedanz, and Mike LaBelle with one of the new series Black Hawk helicopters, May 2009.
(Photo from the author's collection.)

The following day, Mike and I gassed up our Harleys and headed for Minnesota. It was a long ride home and it was taking a toll on Mike. He suffers from some post-Vietnam physical problems that really beat him up when he over-exerts himself. When we got to Windom, Minnesota, around 7:00 p.m. we split up. I headed north on Highway 71 and Mike headed northeast on Highway 60. As luck would have it, he ran into rain before he got home, and spent the next three days in bed.

He still gives me crap about an autograph.

26

THE WAR ON TERROR

THE WAR ON TERROR has been going on now for too many years. Right after the terrorist attacks on the Twin Towers and the Pentagon, President Bush sent American troops to Afghanistan to hunt down the leader of Al Qaeda. All intelligence indicated that he was holed up in the mountainous regions between Afghanistan and Pakistan. Osama bin Laden had claimed that his radical band of Muslims was declaring Jihad on all the infidels of the world.

At the same time, the United Nations was issuing resolution after resolution to the saber-rattling threats from the leader of Iraq. The United States had formerly backed Saddam Hussein over the past number of years. Now he had disassociated himself and his country from the rest of free world. Weapons of mass destruction were of major concern. Sadam Hussien insisted that he didn't have any such weapons, when in fact, the United States had been sending him chemical weapons and technology for years.

In 1990, Sadam Hussein had invaded Kuwait, leading to the Gulf War and the 100-hour defeat of the highly-touted Republic Guard. It took General H. Norman Schwarzkopf and the United States forces just a few days to annihilate Hussein's paper dragon. Unfortunately, then-President George H. Bush reined in the troops. Many people thought that he should have let Schwarzkopf go all the way to Baghdad and take Saddam down. Due to pressures from the UN, President Bush halted the troops at the Iraqi border. A lot of people say that we had no business in

Iraq, but not getting involved and allowing the brutal regime of Saddam Hussein to continue business as usual would have been irresponsible. We all love our freedom here in America. Can we deny the same opportunity to oppressed peoples of the world?

In the spring of 2003, a year-and-a-half after the terrorist attack on September 11, 2001, U.S. troops were sent to Iraq. A new President Bush had been in office for a little over two years, the son of former President George H.W. Bush. After dealing with all the saber-rattling and tough talk by Saddam Hussein, President George W. Bush sent troops to Kuwait, preparing to liberate Iraq of the murderous dictator and his Ba'ath regime. In the beginning, the nation was supportive of this move. All of Congress backed it. However, as the war in Iraq progressed and the number of U.S. servicemen and women killed continued to grow, the American people, and especially our political leaders, once again proved that they don't have the stomach for the fight. As in Vietnam, the politicians and the press were proving to be our worst enemy.

The press, which thrives on sensationalism, once again chose to ignore the great things that our troops were doing for the people of Iraq and Afghanistan, and focused in on anything that would make our troops look like savages. It was okay for the Hodgies to kill our troops and civilian contractors, drag their bodies behind their vehicles, burn them, behead them, and hang them from bridges. But let one of our units be responsible for the deaths of a family of Iraqis who blatantly ran a checkpoint, and the press becomes a self appointed judge, jury, and executioner, never mind the hundreds of innocent women and children the enemy kills almost every day in suicide bombings throughout the Middle East, to say nothing of the cowardly Twin Towers attack in 2001.

The situation was not unlike the North Vietnamese takeover of the ancient city of Hue during Tet of 1968, the NVA murdered over five thousand South Vietnamese without so much as a footnote from the American or the International press. Later that year, when U.S. Army Lieutenant Calley and his men killed what they considered to be enemy civilians in the Village of My Lai, or when pictures of a South Vietnamese officer executing a Viet Cong who had killed family members of the officer made it in the news all over the world, the press had a heyday. While I do not condone the actions of Lt. Calley and his men, it appears that the American press has a huge double standard when it comes to our First Amendment rights and our military. They seem bent on portraying the U.S. servicemen and women as being the bad guys, when in fact, they are the most compassionate people who have ever served in the Armed Forces.

The prisoners who were supposedly tortured at Abu Ghraib—what a farce. Most of the guys that I knew as young men would hardly have considered a pair of women's panties over their head as torture—once again, compared to the North Vietnamese and Viet Cong treatment of our men who were held captive in Vietnam. Prisoners there were beaten and some were killed while in the hands of the North Vietnamese. Many, including my cousin, Lyle Mackedanz, remain unaccounted for to this day.

The U.S. Army and Marines continually say, "Leave no man behind," but our politicians obviously don't give much sway to that. It seems that those who send men to war do not measure up in integrity and morals to the men and women who sign their names and go off to defend our country and our Constitution. The militant Islamics have judged anyone who does not agree with their radical religious beliefs as infidels, doomed to death. Yet they expect complete tolerance of their ideals and religion.

As Americans, we and the rest of the world hold ourselves to a higher standard. Unfortunately, the enemy almost always fights by a different set of rules, that being, no rules. They know full well that although we may be the superior force on the field of battle, they can tie our hands behind our backs by just using our media against us. Were they concerned about the innocent lives lost in the attacks on the Twin Towers or the Pentagon? I don't think so. Are they concerned when they walk into a marketplace with a suicide bomb and kill dozens of innocent women and children? I think not.

During WWI and WWII, did we concern ourselves with how many civilians died in the bombings of Germany and Japan? Hell no! But today, the enemy continues to hide behind the skirts of women and children, and then we are to blame when there are casualties. We are not a country at war, we are merely a country with its military at war. So long as we can continue to have the young, loyal, dedicated men and women of this country take the brunt, while the rest of us sit around and watch TV, it will always be the same. They (our government) try to be politically correct in everything they say and do. They obviously have never heard that the definition of politically correct is "trying to pick up a turd by the clean end." It just isn't possible.

EPILOGUE

THE SILVER STAR

THIS BOOK HAS BEEN A LONG, difficult project. At times it was seemingly impossible to clear all the hurdles required to get it to print. However, I truly believe that everything happens for a reason. The delays in getting it finished seemed endless. My desire to get my story out continued to burn in my gut.

For thirty-some years, I avoided much contact with anything having to do with my military experience. Then I started searching for some of the guys that I had known during those long ago times. In 2002, my wife and I attended our first reunion of the Big Red One (the 1st Infantry Division) in New Orleans, Louisiana. As years progressed, the groups got larger and more and more Bandidos from Charlie Company 1st Battalion, 16th Infantry Regiment attended the reunions. Many times, the conversation would turn to the big firefight that we had during operation Kentucky Cougar on August 12, 1969. A large number of us were wounded and medivaced out by helicopter.

At some point a few years back, Capt. Ken Costich asked me if I had ever received a Bronze Star for my actions during the many firefights that we were in. I told him that I had a CIB (Combat Infantryman's Badge), an Army Commendation Medal, and two Purple Hearts for wounds received in combat, along with the usual Vietnamese awards that we received for our actions while serving in Vietnam. He asked me if it would be okay for him to do a little checking into it. I told Ken that if he was looking at a Bronze Star for meritorious service, to not bother. From my perspective, every Company Clerk and rear echelon soldier had several of them. The Bronze Star had been cheapened up when it was decided that it should be given out as a meritorious service award when originally it was only given out for valor. Now, the medal when awarded for valor has a 'V' device on it which in effect makes it an entirely more prestigious award.

Ken talked with Phil Greenwell (my company commander during Operation Kentucky Cougar) and Al Herrera (my 1st Sergeant during most of 1969). They decided to look into the possibility of putting in for some medals that would have been awarded back in 1969 if Al Herrera had not been severely wounded and medivaced out on August 12, 1969. Phil Greenwell, at the time a twenty-two-year-old Company Commander, had his hands full trying to keep his company combat-effective with all of the casualties that we had taken on that day. I'm sure that worrying about who should receive recognition for their individual actions of the day was probably not of high priority at the time. While many of us were medivaced out on that day, Phil had to make sure that the platoon leaders, platoon sergeants, and other slots were filled with the most capable people.

During the three weeks that followed, the Bandidos were in contact with the enemy on pretty much a daily basis. Capt. Greenwell himself lost three command tracks destroyed by RPGs or land mines. During the period from August 9, 1969 through September 6, 1969, the Bandidos had thirty tracks (APCs) combat-lost. Al Herrera was sent to Japan, and then back to the States to recover from his wounds. I went to the 12th Evac Hospital in Cu Chi where they removed most of the shrapnel from my cheek, neck, shoulder, back and right hand. After a few days at Cu Chi, I was transferred to an Air Force-run convalescent hospital in Cam Rahn Bay.

Ken, Al, and Phil started working on things and after they had each put their information down on paper, with plans of submitting papers for a Bronze Star with a "V" device for me, they decided that my actions of that day appeared to be worthy of a

Silver Star. They also decided that two others should be recognized with Silver Stars and two more with the Bronze Star with "V" device. Ken and Phil also put Al Herrera in for a Silver Star.

Over the past two-and-a-half years, I think that each of us tried not to get our hopes up too high. The odds of getting this through forty years later were pretty slim. However, with the determination of Ken and Phil, each hurdle was eventually cleared. A General from our chain of command was required to sign off on these awards. Locating such a person seemed to be a daunting task as most of our General Officers had already passed on. Finally, in the early spring of 2011, Phil Greenwell managed to locate Major General (retired) Albert Milloy. After talking with the General's wife, Phil received a call back from the General stating that he would be honored to sign the required papers to advance these awards to the next level. With that done, Congressman Benjamin Chandler from Kentucky was able to sponsor the requests, and they were expedited. In August 2011, I was notified that the award was approved. Needless to say, I was very pleased. Phil told me that Silver Star awards were approved for Al Herrera, Melvin McElreath, Doug Ludlow, and me, along with Bronze Stars with the "V" device for Roger Haynie and Steve Biernacke. The awards were all on the desk of Congressman Chandler in Lexington, Kentucky.

This being an extremely rare happening, for six members of one Infantry Company to be receiving these high awards for valor, all from the same action, was a very big deal. The 1st Infantry Division headquarters in Fort Riley, Kansas, and the 1st Battalion, 16th Infantry out of Fort Riley were notified. Most of the 1st Battalion, 16th Infantry (Iron Rangers) were deployed to Afghanistan, due to come home around the middle of January 2012. Plans were initiated to have an awards ceremony at Fort Riley at some time after the Iron Rangers returned from their deployment. Around Thanksgiving Day, the advanced party returned to Fort Riley, lending hopes that the main force would be close behind them. The word we were receiving was that it would take place at Fort Riley around the end of February when LTC James Smith, Battalion Commander for the Iron Rangers, relinquished his command in a change of command ceremony at Fort Riley.

With all of this hinging on so many unknowns, I requested that my award be sent to me, so that I would actually have it in my hands. I guess that after all the years of waiting, I was kind of anxious to have it in my possession. I inquired as to whether or not it might be appropriate for us to have a local presentation of the award during our Veteran's Day observance in Willmar on November 12. Having been reassured that there would be no conflicts, I turned things over to Jon Lindstrand and my wife, Janet. They contacted several friends and family members about the possibility of attending a ceremony. The response was fantastic. While I was somewhat hesitant to proceed, a good friend and former Navy Corpsman who had served with the Marine Corps in Vietnam, fondly known by his friends as Sailor Doc, contacted me. He stated that this was the best news that he had heard from or about Vietnam in over forty years. He said, "Mack, this isn't just about you, this is for every Vietnam Vet that knows you and you need to do this thing." With that little gentle boot in the rear, I told Jon and Janet to go ahead.

Another longtime friend of mine had just retired from the Minnesota National Guard after thirty-nine years of service, the last thirteen as a Command Sergeant Major. Doug Hanson and I go way back. In 1972, while attending vocational school in Willmar, Minnesota, Doug was expecting to be drafted. I encouraged Doug to explore other alternatives. Having been drafted in 1968 and spending a year in the Infantry in Vietnam, it was not high on my list of recommended things to do. Doug looked at his options, and decided to enlist in the Minnesota National Guard. He made the very best of his time with the National Guard, progressing through the ranks to the highest Non-Commissioned Officer rank as a Command Sergeant Major. To say that 'he done me proud' would be a gross understatement.

When the time came to determine who I wanted to pin my Silver Star on me at the ceremony, it was never in doubt. I couldn't see any reason to allow some politician or other local military person whom I barely knew to share that special moment. Doug retired from the Minnesota National guard in July 2011. Janet and I were honored to be present at his retirement ceremony in Roseville, Minnesota. On November 12, 2011, over four hundred and fifty friends, relatives, and others assembled at the Willmar War Memorial Auditorium to witness the informal presentation of the Silver Star to me. Special guest, CSM (Ret.) Bill Ryan, flew up from Melbourne, Florida, to partake in the special day. Jon Lindstrand officiated the program and CSM (Ret.) Doug Hanson called the group to attention for the reading of the orders, after which time he pinned the Silver Star on my DMOR jacket. It was a proud moment.

My wife, Janet, got up and addressed the audience, which really surprised me as she had not done much public speaking prior to that date. Then, Jeff Seeber (Sailor Doc) presented me with a beautiful plaque honoring my achievement. CSM (Ret.) Bill Ryan presented my wife with a dozen roses and then, in some French custom from his WWII days, he came over and planted a kiss on my cheeks. Needless to say, I was not expecting that, but the crowd got a big kick out of it.

I told the crowd that for me to be receiving this on that day, with each of them present, meant more to me than if I would have received it forty-two years prior while lying in hospital bed in Vietnam. It was a day that I will not soon forget.

Sometime in January 2012, we were notified that the official awards presentation ceremony would take place at the headquarters of the 1st Battalion, 16th Infantry Regiment in Fort Riley, Kansas, on March 9. Janet and I had left Minnesota around the end of January heading for Arizona, so we would be making the journey back up to Kansas for the big doings. With Ken Costich living in Tucson, Arizona, we decided that we would drive up to Kansas together. Ken drove up and picked us up and we headed up through the Salt River Canyon in northeast Arizona and on through New Mexico and the Texas panhandle. We made it to Guymon, Oklahoma, and spent the night. We rolled in to Junction City, Kansas, around three o'clock in the afternoon.

On the afternoon of March 9, 2012, a formal ceremony was held at Battalion HQ of the 1st Battalion, 16th Infantry at Fort Riley, LTC James Smith officiating. BG Donald M. MacWillie did the honors of pinning the awards on those of us being recognized that day. Along with the awards for the 'Nam vets, a young Afghan vet named Brian Jergens was awarded his Purple Heart for serious wounds that he received during his tour of duty with the Battalion. The room was filled with family, friends, and soldiers as the presentations were made. Needless to say, it was a proud day for all.

GLOSSARY OF TERMS

ACR—Armored Cavalry Regiment, as in "the 11th ACR".

A.I.T.—Advanced Infantry Training

AK-47—Russian- and Chinese-made personal automatic rifle, 7.62 caliber.

AO—Area of Operation

APC—Armed Personnel Carrier, also known as a 'track'

ARTY—Artillery

ARVN—Army of the Republic of Vietnam (South Vietnam)

ASAP—As soon as possible

AVLB—Armored Vehicle Launched Bridge

B-52's—U.S. long-range bombers. (Dropped large loads of bombs from 35,000 feet)

Baby San—young boy or girl

Bandido Charlie Six—Our Company Commander's call sign

Battle Rattle—Body armor and field gear, (Iraq/Afghanistan)

BDG—Brigade (as in the 4th Brigade)

Blanket Party—a means of dealing with a soldier who during basic and A.I.T. tended to get their entire platoon in trouble. During the night, a blanket was thrown over the culprit and then several others would beat him with a sock filled with bar soap. This usually didn't have to happen more than once.

BN—Battalion (as in the 1st Battalion, 16th Infantry Regiment)

Captain—Next rank after 1st Lieutenant. (Usually served as Company Commander or Staff officers.)

C-Rats—C-Rations/canned meals

CIB—Combat Infantryman's Badge

Civvies—Civilian clothes

Claymore—U.S. anti-personnel mine

CO—Commanding Officer, also known as "the Old Man"

Commo—short for "communications"

Concertina wire—rolls of razor edged wire that we would use to secure our base camps. It came in a coil about three feet high and spread out like a concertina.

Cu hoi—Give up, surrender.

DD-214—Military separation document, showing home of record, type of service, medals and citations received, type of discharge, etc.

DEROS—Date estimated returned over seas. (Going home)

Di An—pronounced "Ze-on", one of the major U.S. bases just northeast of Saigon. Rear Headquarters for the 1st Infantry Division.

DIV—Division, as in 1st Infantry Division, 9th Infantry Division, etc.

Di di mau—Get out of here, go away, move quickly, etc.

Dust-off—Medical evacuation, usually by helicopter, same meaning as medevac

Dress Greens—Formal uniform, worn only on special occasions

Eagle flight—moving troops into combat via helicopter

EM—Enlisted men, ranking as Private E-1 through E-9

EM Club—Enlisted men's club. A building serving cold beer, etc., designated for the lower-ranking enlisted soldiers.

Extra board—List of employees who didn't have enough seniority to hold a regular assigned job.

ETS—Estimated time of separation from the service.

Fatigues—Army uniform worn for everyday duty

Fifty—The fifty-caliber machine gun found on most armored vehicles

Firefight—Ground combat, battle with the enemy

FNG—F---in' new guy

Forty-five—Automatic pistol, forty-five-caliber, carried by officers and some enlisted men

FSB—Fire Support Base, usually occupied by artillery with Infantry support and protection.

GI—Government Issue, also short for an American soldier.

Grunt—an Army Infantryman or Marine who was out in the field, doing ambushes, patrols, etc.

GP medium—a medium sized, general purpose army tent.

HHC—Headquarters and headquarters company

Hoi Chanh—a Viet Cong or NVA soldier who had surrendered and was now working with the U.S. and South Vietnamese as a Kit Carson scout.

Hot LZ—Helicopter landing zone that was under gunfire from the enemy.

HQ—Headquarters

Inf.—Infantry

Jody—The guy back home that one's wife or girlfriend was supposedly stepping out with.

Khakies—Uniform worn for semi-dress occasions

KIA—Killed in action

Kit Carson scout—Usually a former VC or NVA soldier who had Chu Hoi'd and come over to our side.

Klick—unit of measurement: one kilometer or approximately five-eighths of a mile.

KP—kitchen patrol, usually assigned to lower ranking enlisted men for screwing up.

Legs—Dismounted infantry soldiers.

Lai Khe—pronounced "Lie Kay." Forward operating base for the 1st Infantry Division, approximately forty miles north of Saigon. Also the rear base for the 1st Battalion, 16th Infantry.

LT—Lieutenant, junior grade officers, 2nd Lt., then 1st Lt. (Often served as platoon leaders and company level executive officers)

LTC—Lieutenant Colonel (Usually served as Battalion Commanders, or upper level staff officers, etc)

LP—Listening post. (Usually a three-man team, outside the wire; provided early warning to FSB, or NDP.)

LRRP—Long range recon patrol.

LZ—Landing Zone, drop-off point for Eagle flights

M-16—American-made 223-caliber personal automatic weapon.

M-60—American-made 7.62 millimeter squad machine gun.

Ma Deuce—U.S. fifty-caliber machine gun

Mama San—Woman

MASH—Mobile Army Surgical Hospital

MACV—Military Assistance Command, Vietnam. (They worked as advisors to the South Vietnamese military.)

Mech—Mechanized unit, equipped with APC's and often with tanks assigned to them.

Med-Caps—U.S. Army medics providing medical assistance to the local population.

Medevac—Medical Evacuation

MIA—Missing in action

MOS—Military Occupational Specialty

MP—Military Police

MPC—Military Payment Certificates, (U.S. Government-issued funny money used in place of greenback dollars, which were illegal for the troops to have in their possession in 'Nam.)

NCO—Non-Commissioned Officer

NCO Club—A place where Non-Commissioned Officers (sergeants, for example) could go to have a beer. The lower-enlisted ranks were not allowed in.

NDP—Night Defensive Perimeter

Number one—Okay, the best, good

Number ten—Not good

NVA—North Vietnamese Army

Old hats—Railroad employees with seniority.

OJT—On-the-job training

OPCON—Attached to another unit for specific operation

Papa San—Man, father

Piasters—Vietnamese money

POW—Prisoner of war

PCR-25—a squad-issued field radio, also known as the "Prick-25"

PFC—Private First Class, rank E-3 (In 'Nam, PFCs were riflemen, machine gunners, RTOs, or many other assigned positions with-in the squad)

Pogie bait—Donuts, candy bars, cigarettes, and other forbidden foods during basic training.

PTSD—Post-Traumatic Stress Disorder, symptoms dealing with having been involved with or witnessing a traumatic situation. During WWII it was referred to as Shell Shock.

PX—Post exchange. Store

Reveille—Wake-up call for the troops

Rome plows—large caterpillars used by U.S. Army engineers to clear areas of jungle. (They were equipped with 'kits' made in a little town north of Atlanta, Georgia, called Rome. The kits consisted of a heavy duty stinger blade, driver cages, etc.)

RPG—Rocket-propelled grenade (anti-tank, anti-personnel VC/NVA weapon)

RTO—Radio/telephone operator

R & R—Rest and Relaxation (a five-day period to get out of 'Nam)

San pan—small Vietnamese watercraft

Sapper—A person who specializes in infiltration and explosives.

Sgt.—Sergeant, rank E-5. (In 'Nam, infantry sergeants were usually squad leaders)

SKS—Chinese-made automatic rifle carried by some VC and NVA, (also came in bolt action models)

SSGT—Staff Sergeant, rank E-6 (In 'Nam, Infantry SSGTs were usually platoon sergeants)

Short-timer—Someone nearing the end of his tour of duty.

SITREP—Situation report. Usually given over the radio.

SOP—Standard Operating Procedure

SPC 4—Enlisted rank of Specialist E-4

Tank—Large, armored track-type vehicle, often attached to Mechanized Infantry units.

Tet—The Vietnamese New Year

The "Old Man"—The ranking officer in a company or battalion

The "'World"—Home, the U.S.A.

Thump gun—M-79 grenade launcher, looked like a sawed-off shotgun with a big hole in the end of the barrel

TNT—Dynamite

Track—Armed Personnel Carrier, M113A,

VA—Veterans Administration, the national organization charged with serving our nations veterans.

WIA—Wounded in action

GLOSSARY OF NAMES

Alley, Lee—Chapter 23 (Bandido Charlie Six, 5th of 60th)

Ardoin, Kristie—Chapter 20 (Mrs. Phil Ardoin)

Ardoin, Phil (Norman)—Chapter 20 (Bandido)

Argenzio, Joe—Chapter 23 (D-Day vet, deceased)

Arnold, Phil—Chapter 20 (Bandido)

Arnold, Sandy—Chapter 20 (Mrs. Phil Arnold)

Askew, Michael (Doc)—Chapters 19 and 20 (Alpha 1st of the 16th medic)

Baron, Douglas K.—Chapter 19 (Bandido, KIA)

Barouski, Robert—Chapter 8 (Bandido XO)

Baseman, Dale—Chapter 16 (hometown friend, deceased)

Bauman, Brook—Chapter 24 (David Staab's niece)

Beiderstad, Clarence—Chapter 16 (instructor at Willmar Vo-Tech, deceased)

Bell, Gary—Chapter 1 (high school classmate, deceased)

Biernacki, Steve—Chapter 20 and Epilogue (Bandido 4th platoon)

Betancourt, Adeline—Chapter 20 (Mrs. Art Betancourt)

Betancourt, Art—Chapter 20 (WWII vet, deceased)

Blake, David—Chapter 1 (high school friend)

Bosveld, Marvin—Chapter 20 (Rachel's father)

Bosveld, Rachel—Chapter 20 (Iraq, KIA)

Bretch, Bernie—Chapter 2 (friend from Glencoe)

Brooks, Carol—Chapter 25 (Mrs. Vincent Brooks)

Brooks, Vincent—Chapter 25 (Commanding General, 1st Infantry Division)

Brouwer, Don—Chapter 7 (2nd platoon, Bandido)

Burkhart, Sgt.—Chapter 11 (Bandido)

Bush, Pres. George H.W.—Chapter 26

Bush, Pres. George W.—Chapter 26

Cain, Ryan—Chapter 24, (NG soldier, killed in auto accident while home on leave)

Calley, William—Chapters 16 and 26, (My Lai massacre)

Cassels, Kenneth—Chapters 9, 11, and 20 (Former Battalion Commander, 1st of the 16th)

Cassels, Peggy—Chapter 20 (Mrs. Kenneth Cassels)

Chaffin, Ed—Chapter 20 (Bandido)

Chandler, Benjamin—Epilogue (Congressman from Kentucky who pushed our awards through Congress)

Cheney, Wes—Chapter 25 (past Bandido Charlie Six, Fort Riley)

Christensen, Jim—Chapter 1 (high school classmate)

Costich, Kenneth J. II—Chapters 8, 9, 10, 19, 23, and epilogue (Former Bandido Charlie Six)

Day, David—Chapter 24 (Montevideo NG unit, KIA in Iraq)

DeLaFuentes, Pete—Chapter 22 (Bandido)

DeLaurie, Pat—Chapter 11 (2nd platoon Bandido, wounded on August 10, 1969)

De'Oliva—Chapter 9 (Bandido)

Dobson—Chapter 3 (A.I.T. at Fort Lewis)

Dunsmore, Chris—Chapter 24 (Patriot Guard Assistant Ride Captain)

Emmons, Ed—Chapters 8, 12, and 13 (Bandido, deceased)

Farley, Johnny—Chapter 7 (Bandido)

Feeler, Vernon—Chapter 23 (Bandido)

Finkel, David—Chapter 22 (author, *The Good Soldiers*)

Garner, Larry A.—Bandido who gave his all

Gedda, Rebecca—Chapter 19, (staff writer at the *Collinsville Herald Journal*)

Goldberg, Sherwood (Woody)—Chapters 8, 20, and 22 (Bandido Charlie Six, in Vietnam December 1968—March 1969)

Goldenstein, Bruce—Chapter 14 (brother to Greg)

Goldenstein, Gregory (Goldie)—Chapters 7, 8, 10, 11, 14, and 19 (Bandido, 2nd platoon, deceased)

Gore, Jerry—Chapter 19 (Bandido)

Greenwell, Eloise—Chapter 20 (mother of Captain Phillip J. Greenwell, deceased)

Greenwell, Linda—Chapters 20 and 22 (Mrs. Phillip J. Greenwell)

Schuft, Chuck—Chapters 4 and 19 (high school classmate)

Schuft, LuWayne (Butch)—Chapters 4, 5, 13, and 19, (hometown friend, Chuck's brother, 'Nam vet, deceased)

Schwarzkopf, H. Norman—Chapter 26 (General, Desert Storm, deceased)

Scotty—Chapter 23, (Patriot Guard member, bagpiper)

Seeber, Candice—Chapter 24 (Mrs. Jeff Seeber)

Seeber, Jeff (Sailor Doc)—Chapter 24 and epilogue (Navy Corpsman with the Marines in 'Nam, friend)

Shay, Charlie—Chapter 23 (D-Day vet, DMOR)

Skold, Brian—Chapter 24 (Iraq war casualty, deceased)

Silvia, Dennis—Chapter 24 (Bandido)

Smith, LTC James—Epilogue, (past Battalion Commander, 1st of the 16th Infantry)

Squires, Capt. Michael—Chapter 22 (former Bandido Charlie Six, Fort Riley)

Staab, Cindy—Chapter 24 (David Staab's mother)

Staab, David—Chapter 24 (Iraq War casualty, deceased)

Staab, Mike—Chapter 24 (David Staab's father)

Stelzreide, Stacy—Chapter 4 (author's niece)

Sterling, David—Chapter 2, (1st of the 16th Iraq, 2004, WIA, Silver Star recipient)

Taylor, Charlie—Chapter 23 (Bandido)

Tessaro, Michael—Chapters 7, 19, 20, and 21, (Bandido, friend, Vietnam, KIA)

Tessaro, Mike—Chapter 19 (Michael Tessaro's father, deceased)

Tessaro (Holst), Roseanne—Chapter 19 (Michael Tessaro's sister)

Thompson, Gilbert (Doc)—Chapter 20 (Bandido medic, friend, DMOR)

Thompson, Janeen—Chapter 20 (Mrs. Gil Thompson, friend, DMOR)

Timmerman, Jason—Chapter 24 (Iraq, KIA)

Van Der Hagen, Emily—Chapter 22 (Richard Martinson's wife, friend.)

Wangerin, Mike—Chapters 9, 12, and 14 (brother-in-law, Vietnam veteran)

Warren, John—Chapters 19 and 21 (Vietnam vet, Marine, WIA, VA counselor, friend)

Wesley, Butch—Chapter 25 (Vietnam Vet, Marine, WIA, friend)

Wence, Scott—Chapter 22 (former Bandido Charlie Six, Iraq and Fort Riley)

Wilhelm, Kaiser—Chapter 1

Wilhelmy, Rick—Chapter 25 (Iraq vet, friend)

Winslow, Jeanie—Chapter 20 (Mrs. Wendelin Winslow)

Winslow, Wendelin (Wendy)—Chapters 5, 7, 8, 20, and 23 (Bandido Charlie Six, Vietnam, May 1968—December 1968)

Witte, Kevin—Chapter 24 (Iraq, KIA)

Zachar, Frank—Chapters 22 and 23 (former Battlion Commander, 1st of the 16th, Fort Riley and Iraq)

Zachar, Frankie—Chapter 22 (Frank and Michelle's son)

Zachar, Michelle—Chapter 22 (Mrs. Frank Zachar)

Zachar, Wolfie—Chapter 22 (Frank and Michelle's son)

Zemple, Gene—Chapters 19 and 23, (Bandido, 1st platoon, deceased)

Zemple, Jeanie—Chapter 23 (Mrs. Gene Zemple)

Ron's medals. Top to bottom, left to right: Combat Infantryman's Badge, Silver Star, Purple Heart, Purple Heart with first oak leaf, Army Commendation Medal, Good Conduct Medal, National Defense Medal, U.S. Vietnam Service Medal with four campaign stars, RVN Gallantry Medal, RVN Civil Action Honor Medal, Vietnam Campaign Medal with 1960 device, Army Presidential Unit Citation, Army Meritorious Unit Citation, Vietnam Presidential Unit Citation.

ABOUT THE AUTHOR

Ron Mackedanz was born in Hutchinson, MN. on June 26, 1948, the second child in what was to be a family of eight children (five boys and three girls). Ron grew up watching his Dad and many other WWII vets march proudly in the Memorial Day parade each year in the quaint little town of Hutchinson. Ron attended public school and graduated in June, 1966. He promptly found work and after a few months of bouncing around from one low-paying job to another, Ron headed out to seek fame and fortune in sunny California.

In April 1968, just days before his cousin Lyle came up as MIA in Vietnam, Ron received his draft notice. He and Janet went back to Minnesota and in May, Ron entered the U.S. Army. After the two years in the Army were through, Ron took advantage of the GI Bill and got a degree in Marketing Management. A few years later he returned to school and pursued a degree in Accounting.

Ron and his wife, Janet have three daughters and five grandchildren. They are retired and Ron spends much of his time working on many issues concerning veterans and their families.

Ron spent one year in Vietnam with Bandido Charlie Company 1st Battalion, 16th Infantry (mechanized) as an infantryman with the famous Big Red One. He received the Combat Infantryman's Badge, the Silver Star for valor in combat, two Purple Hearts for wounds received in combat, the Army Commendation medal, the Republic of South Vietnam Cross of Gallantry and numerous other medals and ribbons awarded individually and as a member of an outstanding unit.

In 2005, Ron was recognized as a Distinguished Member of the 16th Infantry Regiment.

Distributed by:
Kasota Lake Productions
P.O. Box 251
Kandiyohi, MN 56251

Please e-mail Ron Mackedanz at bandidomack@gmail.com in
order to purchase additional copies.